DENIS GUERRA

Rebus Da Vinci

Facebook

https://www.facebook.com/rebusdavinci/

DEDICATED TO

I never had any doubts about who this book would be dedicated to.

My dedication is intended as a very special thank you to two people who warm my heart every day.

Exceptionally and incredibly selfless, they are the angels who have made my life a dream.

In a thousand ways they have supported me and in another thousand helped me; they have taught me to live and to walk, to look and to talk, to smile and to cry.

I can hardly find words to express my gratitude to them: they have devoted their lives to my happiness.

I have tried to do my best to repay them for everything they have given me.

To them I dedicate this book, as ever with immense gratitude and sincere respect.

With great love and admiration,

Your son.

CHARITY

A part of the proceeds from this story will be donated to the "Milky Association", a humanitarian association helping poor children and teenagers throughout the world.

milkyassociation.org

Website:

www.milkyassociation.org

PREFACE

"Discovery consists of seeing what everybody has seen and in thinking what nobody has thought."

Albert Szent-Györgyi, 1893-1986, Hungarian scientist

INTRODUCTION

Have you ever wondered how the mind of a genius works?

What myriad thoughts and ideas weave through such reasoning?

Imagine succeeding in deciphering a series of messages cleverly concealed in Leonardo da Vinci's manuscripts!

Illustrious scholars have examined his codexes in search of hidden concepts and undisclosed intuitions, but few have considered his greatest passion: his rebuses.

The Renaissance genius would test his students by hiding symbols and words on different pages; only those closest to their master's way of thinking were able to recognize and use these elements to compose rebuses and to find their solution.

500 years after Leonardo's death, a new student begins investigating his codexes, resolving centuries-old rebuses through remarkable feats of lateral thinking.

Denis Guerra

Rebus Da Vinci

Chapter One

8 december 1984

8 december 1984 (mirrored)

"Imagination is more important than knowledge."

Albert Einstein, 1879-1955, German physicist

"Leonardo, make a wish and blow out the candles" Sophie whispers to her beloved son.

A great Black Forest gateau, almost too big for those ten candles.

A gang of excited, happy kids celebrating with their friend, piles of gifts related to the all-consuming passion that has earned him a reputation as a Lego genius. He has that natural talent for creating things with extreme facility.

Models of all kinds take shape in his fingers, with no limits to his creativity.

He is enthralled by the construction game providing him with endless possibilities of satisfying his intuitive and imaginative side.

Fiery red gift paper with a big white bow; while it might not be the biggest, it is certainly the present that has captured his attention. In the midst of all those predictable packages it is the only one with any mystery.

Leonardo delicately unties the soft ribbon.

He has no idea about what is inside and the fact that the gift would somehow change his life, delivering a message that only many years later would he succeed in deciphering.

With trembling hands he looks for the exact spot to unwrap the package without damaging the paper. He wants to keep intact everything that will remind him of that fantastic tenth birthday.

It proves to be a high-tech black digital alarm clock.

*** *** ***

By sunset the usual calm has returned to the house.

The guests have left and Leonardo is closeted in his bedroom contemplating the gifts he has received, absorbed in his creative world; it is a special evening and he wants to spend it alone, to enjoy its intensity to the full.

Tired, but thoroughly satisfied, he lies down beside the alarm clock glowing on the bedside table.

He is already familiar with all its features, a quick glance at the instructions and everything is promptly memorized: the newcomer has no further secrets and is ready to do its duty.

Tonight the absence of light in his bedroom does not frighten him; the red light from the display prevents darkness from taking the upper hand.

Despite his tiredness, he has trouble falling asleep: his eyes are drawn to those digital numbers.

The strong light starts to become irritating and prevents him from sleeping.

What was supposed to be a fantastic gift is rapidly turning sour.

Inexplicably, despite the irritation, he cannot help staring at and studying the clock, feeling deeply attracted to the numbers that seem to be concealing something from him.

He watches the minutes passing by, the number of segments lighting up depending on the time. Lying quite still, his gaze spellbound, he finds the lucidity to ask himself one of those rather odd questions typical of Leo:

"What time indicated on the display lights up the most segments?"

Sighing, he completes his own question "...and is therefore the brightest?"

His gaze returns to the alarm clock.

A brief study of the composition of the figures is all he needs.

"The number eight is the most complete!" he concludes, noting that seven segments light up to compose the figure.

Starting out with this basic consideration, straightforward reasoning allows him to quickly define the crucial time that glitters with more determination and intensity.

Leo smiles, pleased with this peculiar discovery and within a few minutes he finally falls into a deep sleep.

His birthday is over and with it the day of the Immaculate Conception; Leonardo has unknowingly received an encoded message, the real meaning of which he will only one day understand.

Chapter Two

8 december 2007
<hr>
8 december 2007

"He seemed to those about him as one listening to a voice,
silent for other men."

Walter Pater, 1839-1894, English essayist and critic

According to the Gospels, Jesus was thirty-three when he was crucifed, the final event of his earthly life prior to his resurrection.

Today Leo is celebrating this significant milestone in an elegant restaurant with fine cuisine and very relaxed atmosphere.

No friends on this occasion, but a quiet dinner with his beloved parents and sister.

Sophie, his mother, is a small woman with a strong and very determined personality who has devoted her life to the family.

His father, Luca, is a hard worker with an excellent mind and a lover of nature from whom Leo has inherited tenacity and a winning personality.

His sister Maria is the artist of the family.

Dinner is over and replete with the excellent food the guests linger, happily chatting.

Theirs has always been a very close, joyful family.

The candles warm the atmosphere.

Sophie and Luca smile with a satisfied air, enjoying the deep, positive sensations.

The ritual of the giving of gifts draws near and according to a long-established custom it takes place after dessert and before coffee.

The guest of honour's curiosity is palpable; his relatives know his mood: this is one of the few moments they enjoy total control, with Leo a temporary hostage.

The bulkiest gift is easily recognizable, the guest of honour's oldest hobby. "Wonder what that might be!" he comments with gentle irony, as he catches his mother's eye.

Sophie looks at him and without waiting for her son to unwrap the package she exclaims:

"We decided to play it safe!"

It is the latest creation from the Danish construction kit manufacturer, marketed as Lego Technics, the most complex to assemble.

Leo has never stopped creating and inventing and is always in search of novelties and puzzles to analyze: the child in him keeps on playing.

In this respect he resembles the person he thinks of as his master, described by none other than Sigmund Freud in the following terms:

"In many ways the great Leonardo da Vinci remained childish throughout his life, he continued to play in adulthood, something that on occasion was disturbing and incomprehensible in the eyes of his contemporaries."

*** *** ***

On the table remains an unknown factor, wrapped in bright, fiery red gift paper with a big white bow: déjà vu.

His mind takes him back in time to twenty-three years earlier when he received his inseparable alarm clock whose numbers still glow on his bedside table today.

A card precedes the giving of the gift, its hand-written words expressing the sincerity of the message:

"Dear brother, your name is a guarantee of creativity. Keep on expressing it without chains, give full rein to your ingenuity and always believe in your talent. With great respect and love, Maria"

Leonardo's eyes light up, and visibly moved, he thanks his sister for the thought.

He is very close to her, certainly more so than he reveals.

Wrapped in the gift paper he finds a book.

"The Life of Leonardo da Vinci" he exclaims, reading the title on the cover.

He picks up Maria's card and he reads the message again out loud in front of the cleared table.

"… Your name is the guarantee of creativity…"

The clear association with the name of his master, the greatest genius of all time, moves him.

After having thanked his sister, he quickly leafs through the first pages.

The book intends to guide the reader along a journey, exploring the life of the genius.

484 pages of pure culture and knowledge; well structured and richly illustrated with his works, his creations, his codexes and his notes.

In the first pages the book introduces the great da Vinci thus:

"... an artist and a universal scientist considered the greatest genius of all humanity."

*** *** ***

The day draws to a close, Leo feels satisfied; days spent with his family relax him and help recharge his batteries.

He goes to bed and focuses on his old alarm clock.

The book he received is on the bedside table, he observes it doubtfully, aware that he is very tired and he would only be reading for a few minutes.

Unable to resist, he reaches out his hand and picks it up.

After a short but careful study of the interesting cover, portraying a number of the artist's works, he opens it by pure chance right in the middle, at page 242.

"A Double Masterpiece" is the title of the chapter and in the centre of the page is one of the artist's most famous works.

The Virgin of the Rocks

It portrays Maria surrounded by the infants Jesus, Saint John and an angel.

It is an oil painting on canvas realized between 1483 and 1486 and is today conserved in the Louvre in Paris.

It is one of Da Vinci's most important works, a chain of events leading to two copies being produced, and was commissioned by the Confraternity of the Immaculate Conception.

Leonardo stops reading and raises his eyes to heaven.

"The Immaculate Conception, the 8th of December, my birthday!" he realises incredulously.

A remarkable coincidence. As he closes the book in astonishment his creativity catapults him along an unusual path of reasoning.

For his thirty-third birthday he receives a book about his master's life, he opens it precisely in the middle and by a curious coincidence the first paragraph brings him back to that same date, the day of the Immaculate Conception, the 8th of December.

Pure chance or a message?

Deep sleep has already carried him away, with the book as a companion on his pillow.

Chapter Three

Leonardo Da Vinci

Leonardo Da Vinci

"Leonardo da Vinci had predicted that to the extent to which truth was more widely known, consensus would have taken the place of individual opinions."

Thomas Mann, 1875-1955, German writer and essayist

Leonardo da Vinci was born on the 15th of April 1452 in Vinci, Italy, and died on the 2nd of May 1519 in Amboise, France.

A man of immeasurable intelligence and talent, he fully embodied the universalist spirit of the Italian Renaissance, achieving the highest forms of expression in the most diverse fields of art and knowledge.

He was a painter, a sculptor, an architect, an engineer, a mathematician, an anatomist, a musician and an inventor.

He is regarded as one of humanity's greatest geniuses.

To be a scholar of da Vinci's writings entails facing a huge quantity of material, that to say the least can be discouraging, not only in terms of its quantity but also due to its great variety and the relative difficulties of interpretation.

Then, of course, there are the specific problems his manuscripts present, which would already be difficult enough to understand were they not written in Leonardo's unique style.

Legend has it that he was a kind of technological dreamer, an inventor of devices that could not be realized by his patrons.

Despite the breadth of his scientific studies and enduring public interest, he remains an enigmatic, elusive figure, quite capable of deceiving us every time we examine his works or try to observe him from a new perspective.

None of his predecessors or contemporaries produced anything comparable, nor do we know of anyone from the following centuries who can be compared to him.

The fertility of his imagination was such that, while resting on solid empirical foundations, it led him to places that only a few among the most fanciful artists and philosophers have ever explored.

Leonardo da Vinci, self-portrait

Of his entire output over nine thousand pages of notes remain, all characterized by his unmistakable mirror writing, reading from right to left.

Following Leonardo's death, this vast quantity of manuscripts was subjected to fire, theft and acts of vandalism.

When he died, he left all his writings to his faithful disciple Francesco Melzi, who preserved them carefully, but when Melzi in turn died his heirs permitted the gradual dispersal of this incomparably important heritage.

Unaware of their importance, they initially stored the writings in an attic and then began to give them away or to sell them cheaply to friends or collectors.

The seventeenth-century sculptor Pompeo Leoni played a significant role in the reordering of the papers.

He separated the artistic from the technological drawings and unified the scientific folios, initially transforming the original manuscripts into two great collections: the Atlantic Codex and the Windsor Collection.

Continuing to adopt the same system, Leoni subsequently assembled a further four major files.

Through to the end of the seventeenth century most of the manuscripts were held in the Ambrosiana Library, from where Napoleon had them removed on his arrival in Milan.

By the mid-nineteenth century only part of the collection had been returned to Milan.

Other papers remained in Paris and Spain, where they were not found until the Sixties.

Hence the remarkably broad dispersion of the writings, which are today separated into no less than ten different codexes.

Chapter Four

500 years later

500 years later

"He seemed to his contemporaries to be the possessor of some unsanctified and secret wisdom."

Walter Pater, 1839-1894, English essayist

Numbers are one of Leo's greatest passions.

He is attracted by all that they may hide: sometimes he spends hours studying sequences trying to find a logic, convinced that each has its own meaning.

He analyses any numerical coincidence with a visceral passion, sometimes with the help of paper and pen, repeating over and over series of combinations, searching for alternative solutions that more often than not come to nothing.

The coincidence he found in the book has aroused his curiosity and sparks a journey in search of something, of some dark revelation.

"Why would chance lead me to discover such a coincidence?" he continues to ask himself.

"Is there a message behind this date?" he wonders obsessively.

He has become enraptured by the mysterious Leonardesque style, catapulted into a multi-faceted enigmatic world.

*** *** ***

He sits on the rocking chair under the shelter of the veranda, observing the rain.

It is a cold February afternoon, spring still a distant mirage.

He is particularly thoughtful today, preoccupied by the chance discovery in the book, the significance of which he has yet to unravel.

He raises his eyes and, staring into space, focuses on what he already knows.

With a start he stands up and goes back into the house, leaving the chair rocking.

He climbs the stairs and opens the squeaky hatch leading to the attic.

A dusty box lies in a corner.

He walks over and grabs it firmly.

Returning to the veranda he lays the box on the floor and dusts it off with his hand. After a long sigh, two heartfelt words break the silence.

"Dear Grandad."

His grandfather had died when Leo was only ten years old and all that he left him is contained in that box.

The memories associated with his grandfather all concern his greatest passion, to which the old man had wisely introduced him with incredible tales.

Leo's hands stop; among the objects conserved in the box he has found what he was looking for: a book.

He sits down on the rocking chair and after having brushed the dust off its cover he exclaims:

"Leonardo da Vinci's Life and Manuscripts."

Leo's passion for the Renaissance genius had actually been handed down by his grandfather and those pages recount the life and the works of the most extraordinary mind of all time.

He puts down the "Life" and takes up his sister's gift again.

He reopens it at page 242 and re-reads:

"... the work commissioned by the Confraternity of the Immaculate Conception was to be delivered by the 8th of December 1484..."

This strange coincidence excites his curiosity.

His dear grandfather had told him that it had always been Leonardo Da Vinci's custom to keep to hand a number of sheets of paper for making notes, as with his mind always occupied, he was unable to keep track of all the information he desired, sometimes forgetting important details and appointments. Similarly, Leo's grandfather made use of a small pocket notebook.

He puts a hand into the old box and he finds his grandfather's old notebook with a ballpoint pen attached.

He leafs through the first pages in search of an empty sheet.

The old notes make him smile.

He picks up the pen and in an unattractive but bold script he writes:

"8 December 1484"

As a lover of numbers he looks at what he has written and starts playing around with the figures.

He scribbles a few dates on the paper, trying to make logical connections.

"My God!" he exclaims.

He tears out the page full of dates and starts again on a new one.

He rewrites the date "8 December 1484" and with a steady hand carefully changes the first 4 into a 9.

"1984!" he confirms aloud.

"500 years!"

He repeats with a surprised tone. "Exactly 500 years later!"

He puts down the pen and stops in satisfaction to observe the new date: "8 December 1984".

*** *** ***

The rain keeps on pouring down.

There would be no sun that weekend either, and the forecasts were gloomy in the extreme.

Laying the notebook on top of the book, he goes back in and fetches a blanket from the built-in wardrobe in the hall.

He returns to the chair and rocks thoughtfully.

"8 December 1984", he reconfirms.

There has to be a meaning to the date: there has to be more to the 500-year coincidence.

The blanket is no longer enough, the winter temperature is making itself felt.

He closes the box, puts the two books and the notebook on top of it, folds the blanket and goes back in.

He goes upstairs to his bedroom and, after having carefully placed the box next to the bed, he lies down.

The alarm clock on the bedside table says 18:10.

"Wait!" he cries, as he catches sight of the time.

"The gift!" he grins with a satisfied air observing the digital numbers.

On the 8th of December 1984, his beloved alarm clock had been one of the many gifts he has received, and ever since its digital numbers had accompanied him in the darkness of his bedroom.

And what if there's a clue concealed in that date?

Or even in that sleepless night?

His mind roams.

His thoughts return to the night of his tenth birthday.

The light emitted by those red segments had lit the bedroom, so annoying as not to let him rest, but he remembers that he had stared at them as though hypnotized.

Did those numbers that had captured his gaze have a meaning?

"20:08!" he confirms, remembering the time in question.

The brightest combination of figures illuminating the greatest number of segments.

He had put that odd discovery to one side, but now after so many years maybe it could help, perhaps he would find the real meaning behind it.

He picks up the notebook again and opens it at the page on which he had written the two crucial dates.

He quickly draws the time at the bottom of the sheet, in the unmistakable digital style.

"Nothing!" he exclaims desolately.

He picks up the alarm clock and by pressing a combination of buttons he makes the time on the display appear.

Leonardo scrutinizes those figures, just as he had done twenty-three years before.

A few minutes later a smile creases his face, his eyes light up and with a sure voice he cries:

"It's a date!"

He joyfully strengthens his reasoning by affirming:

"It's not a time but a date, a year, 2008!"

Many years after first making that strange discovery he manages to pin down its true meaning: rather than a time, it is a year.

From the outset his faithful companion had been sincere with him, in its own way it had tried to give him a message that only now was he able to decipher.

The satisfaction of the discovery is short-lived.

"But what can that date mean?"

Leo returns to the maelstrom of his thoughts.

He picks up his pen again and turns the time into the date, simply by cancelling the two dots that divide the hour from the minutes.

A combination of preoccupation and excitement overwhelms him.

"This is the year 2008!" he affirms, proceeding with logic.

In search of confirmation he reaches out a hand toward the bedside table and he grabs his mobile phone.

He presses the right button and brings up the agenda.

"26 February 2008!" he exclaims, observing the calendar.

*** *** ***

The rain tinkles incessantly on the railing of the balcony.

Snuggled down under the duvet he stares at the sheet of paper, mentally summarizing the various steps in the story.

"On the day of my tenth birthday, on the 8th of December 1984, I received a gift with a message that only today, on the 26th of February 2008, can I decode."

"What's the meaning of that message?" he wonders insistently.

What is hidden behind the year 2008?

He tears the page from the notebook, crumples it up and fretfully throws it to the side of the bed, where it lands beneath the poster of the Vitruvian Man hanging opposite the bed, the same drawing reproduced on the cover of his grandfather's book he'd dug out of the box in the attic.

He gaze catches that of the ideal man and for a few moments he remains still and thoughtful.

He places the precious notebook on the bedside table.

He picks up the gift he had received from his sister and goes back to the famous page where his adventure began; who knows if that page held other surprises.

He calmly re-reads the paragraph concerning the famous work, the Virgin of the Rocks, in search of further coincidences.

Besides the date of birth however he cannot find anything else.

In search of a clue he observes the work reproduced on a double-page spread.

Nothing.

Frustrated he puts the book on the pillow and he closes his eyes.

Meanwhile the rain has stopped and the balcony rail is silent.

Perhaps now snow is falling softly, noiselessly.

Leo reaches out his hand and turns off the light.

*** *** ***

Silence reigns in the room, the snow falls heavily and smothers all sound.

Slowly the landscape changes, the old houses grouped around the square seem to huddle together for warmth, while a blanket of snow covers the roofs.

Light filters through the screens from the street lamp illuminating the square with the old fountain.

Leo has trouble falling asleep; his thoughts remain fixed on those pages and on those mysterious coincidences.

Grumpily he turns the light back on.

He fussily adjusts the pillow against the head of the bed and he starts reading again.

He re-reads the paragraph yet again, lingering over the words rather than the meaning of the sentences that he now knows by heart.

"The Confraternity of the Immaculate Conception" he exclaims, recalling the anniversary of his date of birth.

"So what is it? A sect?" he wonders curiously.

He goes over to his small bookcase and takes out an old encyclopaedia.

He leafs through the volume and finds a description:

"… having at its disposal sizeable amounts of money, this powerful, outwardly non-profit confraternity commissioned important works from the most popular painters and sculptors."

"The Virgin of the Rocks" was commissioned from Leonardo da Vinci, to be delivered by the 8th of December 1484.

An absurd thought flashes through his mind.

An idea so surreal that he can hardly even consider it.

"Pure fantasy!" the dreamer decides and vows to abandon what would seem to be an impossible idea.

He stops reading.

He looks at the Vitruvian Man and he asks him defiantly:

"So what's going on?"

Leo smiles, recognising the absurdity of the situation.

After some minutes spent looking at the Ideal Man, waiting for an answer that was never going to come, he decides to allow his imagination free rein.

He finds his pen and on an empty sheet of the notebook he draws up a table composed of two columns of four spaces.

He decides to fill each space of the first column with the following four details:

"Confraternity / Leonardo Da Vinci / 8 December 1484 / Virgin of the Rocks"

Without hesitation he immediately moves on to the second column.

Alongside the first three entries in the first column he writes the following:

"Leonardo da Vinci / Leo / 8 December 2008 /…"

The pen stops, leaving the last box empty.

Leo's embarrassment is caused by what he is thinking but cannot write.

His hand remains motionless on the sheet, lacking the courage to go on.

Confraternity	Leonardo Da Vinci
Leonardo Da Vinci	Leo
8 december 1484	8 december 2008
virgin of the rocks	...

The snow has covered the cobbles of the square and a deafening silence grips the empty streets of the town centre.

The frozen fountain is white all over.

Leo is still hesitating over the last remaining cell.

With a click he retracts the point and places the pen on his pillow.

The alarm clock reminds him that it is 22:35.

It is late, but now he is no longer sleepy.

He continues to scrutinize the poster defiantly.

He plucks up his courage and returns to the notebook.

Almost timidly he summarizes the first column.

"The Confraternity has commissioned from Leonardo da Vinci, to be delivered no later than the 8th of December 1484, the work entitled "The Virgin of the Rocks."

He moves on to the second column and continues whispering.

"Leonardo da Vinci has commissioned from Leo, no later than the 8th of December 2008,..."

Leo stops, not because he has lost his voice, but because there is nothing left to read.

"I must be mad!" he laughs.

"It's impossible, what am I thinking of?" he concludes by closing the notebook.

The situation had begun to become unbearable.

While it is true that he has discovered a series of strange coincidences and connections, any thought of a hypothetical work commissioned from him directly by da Vinci had no logical explanation.

"But then what connection is there with the 8th of December 2008?" he wonders disconsolately.

After a few minutes of discomfort, the desire for understanding prevails on the strength of the fact that his ideas are mere suppositions and subject to no external judgment.

He decides to proceed by way of logical reasoning.

"The 8th of December is my birthday!"

"I will be 34 years old", he continues.

He looks for the notebook lying at the foot of the wardrobe, still open at the page with the two-column table.

In the third cell of the first column he had written:

"8 December 1484".

He turns and picks up the book again.

He searches for the passage where the date is marked and reads:

"... to be delivered no later than the 8th of December 1484..."

He returns to the table and observing the third line of the second column he confirms:

"8 December 2008!"

He stops for a moment and then exclaims:

"... and what is it that I should deliver no later than the 8th of December 2008?"

Leo is thinking feverishly, with a mixture of incredulity and excitement.

Usually when he is unable to resolve a problem he proceeds step by step.

He therefore decides to start again from the beginning and use logic to construct a path to follow.

There is still space below the table he drew in the notebook.

"34" he writes with a steady hand.

He observes that age and he returns to the book.

"Deliver it no later than!" he notes.

His reasoning is simple, almost elementary.

"At the age of 33 I have to present something" he declares.

At that precise moment the clock shows midnight, with the three digital zeros lighting up in red.

The snow continues to fall.

Leo replaces the duvet and adjusts his pillow.

He crosses out the 34 in the notebook and at the bottom he adds:

"33"

He stops, frozen by a thought. A shiver runs the length of his spine

"The age at which Christ died!" he exclaims with some trepidation.

*** *** ***

Leo has a very particular relationship with the church. He is not a practising believer: he prefers to rely on other fundamental theories such as nature and science.

As he sees it these last provide more reliable confirmation of his ideologies.

On the contrary, Sophie is a firm believer and when discussing ecclesiastical matters their differences of opinion are evident.

"Christ was crucified at the age of 33!" he repeats confidently, remembering the Gospel teachings.

The cells in the table now seem less mysterious.

He goes back to the second column and timidly says, "Leonardo da Vinci has commissioned something from me to be delivered at the age of 33."

Absurd as it might appear, the two columns show the same thoughts: two works commissioned within a well-defined timeline.

Confraternity	Leonardo Da Vinci
Leonardo Da Vinci	Leo
8 december 1484	8 december 2008 ~~34~~ 33
virgin of the rocks	...

The eight cells composing the table present only one unknown factor: while the Virgin of the Rocks was the work commissioned from Leonardo da Vinci, what is it that Leo has to present?

His curriculum features no artistic studies, he has no skill in painting, sculpture or art in general.

His passion for Leonardo da Vinci has ensured that he is aware of the master's works, particularly the most famous, but otherwise he is hardly an art expert.

The great genius created numerous inventions, his mind freely ranging through various fields.

What would Leonardo da Vinci have asked of a mere boy born more than 500 years after him?

Taking into consideration the evolution of the world over the last five centuries, how could a man born in 1500 commission a creation for the new millennium?

Among his myriad talents Leonardo da Vinci possessed the gift of prophecy, a quality not always easily accepted by his contemporaries.

They believed the master's remarkable scientific and technological intuitions to be the fruit of an imagination a little too lively.

Just think of some of his creations that anticipated their times by some centuries.

Take his great passion for flight shown in numerous of illustrations and drawings scattered through his manuscripts in which he proposes various prototypes for flying machines.

He made a famous prophecy about the aeroplanes that were first to appear four centuries later: "Terrible flying species will cross the skies, and from there they will attack men and animals, filling the world with blood."

Referring to cars, the prophet Da Vinci spoke of "snorting monsters", able to cover long distances in a short time. They would replace the only means of transport of his own age: horses.

*** *** ***

Leo is left with the book open and his precious notebook showing the two columns.

He can hardly believe all those mysterious connections.

He lifts his head and once again finds himself looking at the poster of the Vitruvian man, da Vinci's representation of perfection.

"Impossible!" he exclaims.

He jumps out of bed, puts on his slippers and runs downstairs.

He turns on the computer.

The seconds waiting for it to start seem like hours.

"It's really true that when you're in a hurry everything seems so slow!" he whispers impatiently.

Eventually the main screen appears.

He clicks on the Internet icon to start the application and keys in the address of a major search engine.

Convinced that he is on the right track, he searches for the following combination: "Vitruvian Man + crucified Christ"

Click!

2,410 results.

Leo sighs and after having drawn his breath, he looks at the results page.

The first short description seems to have already confirmed his expectations.

"Decoding the Vitruvian Man."

He scrolls down quickly with the mouse to the link.

Click!

The page rapidly appears on the monitor.

Leo's eyes open wide.

"Wow!" he exclaims in astonishment.

The figure of the Vitruvian Man appears on the screen in all its glory.

An anatomical representation of the perfect human body, with exemplary proportions, set within both a circle and a square.

The image that remains engraved in the mind of an observer is that of a divinity.

It is believed that the work has become so famous because it mirrors the canons of beauty and perfection of an evolved human being, becoming a contemporary symbol of the sought-after spiritual and corporeal perfection.

Perfectly balanced according to the Renaissance humanistic canon, several sources actually consider it to be the model for the representation of Jesus's body on the cross.

Chapter Five

Rebus

"The secret of creativity is knowing how to hide your sources."

Albert Einstein, 1879-1955, German physicist

Fog smothers that dark evening in early March.

Leonardo is in bed with a bad cold and running a temperature.

The old alarm clock lights up the dim bedroom.

He stares at those enduring red numbers as he had done many years before, the difference now being that he knows their underlying message: the year 2008.

On the bedside table lie the precious books devoted to the genius.

Immersed in his world, he sets in motion the usual train of thoughts.

"Maestro, what is it you want of me?" he eventually asks.

"I'm neither an artist nor a painter, not even a writer!" he thinks ruefully.

"Some kind of task?" he wonders.

Gazing up at his bedroom ceiling, he mentally summarizes the steps that led him to that sentence.

"The alarm clock received as a gift for my tenth birthday, on the 8th of December 1984, conceals a message: the year 2008, when I am 33 years old, the age at which Our Lord was crucified, represented by da Vinci with the Vitruvian Man."

Leonardo goes over these events, continually in search of an element connecting all the pieces, as if it were a rebus.

The student shivers.

He loves deciphering puzzles and discovering hidden combinations, especially if the creator of the mysterious enigma is his guide.

The cover of the book he found in the attic glitters in the darkness of the bedroom.

What if was that the clue?

The old book bequeathed to him by his grandfather and portraying on its cover the Vitruvian Man in all his glory.

Dubiously, he picks up the book again.

"Leonardo da Vinci's Life and Manuscripts", he comments, re-reading the title written in block capitals.

An anthology compiled with a great deal of care, details from his works and his manuscripts being used to describe the prodigy's life faithfully.

The text is divided into three main sections, entitled "Life", "Mystery" and "Inheritance."

The first part is devoted to an understanding of how Leonardo's life unfolded in the cities of Tuscany and Renaissance Italy, through to his last days in France.

The second focuses on the immense aura of mystery that has always surrounded him, that has made him into the character you turn to when you cannot find an explanation for something.

The final section deals with the heritage that da Vinci handed down to us and which is now conserved in various parts of the world.

Leo goes back to the index, albeit without any idea of what he is looking for.

His eyes roam over the numerous titles listed on the two pages among photos and drawings.

One of the genius's most famous works embellishes the table of contents:

The Mona Lisa.

Leo hazes at the picture with a critical eye.

He stops reflecting on Mona Lisa's portrait.

"Too obvious!" he decides firmly.

A remarkable number of studies have in fact been dedicated to this mysterious woman with her thoughtful expression and almost enigmatic hint of a smile.

The painting may rightly be considered as the most famous in the world and has become an icon of painting itself or visual arts in general.

Few other works are so celebrated and so widely reproduced.

Leonardo discards this as a clue, considering it to be too obvious, aware as he is that his master would have made his life much more difficult.

The small photo below shows the village of Vinci, the home of the Ideal Leonardo Da Vinci Museum, an institution devoted to studies of the figure of Leonardo and the complexity of his works.

To one side is a chapter that immediately arouses his curiosity.

"The discovery" the student reads aloud.

"And discovery it is!" he comments, smiling and leafing through the book to page 14.

Having found the right place he begins to read carefully.

"...Discovering the countless mysteries that are still concealed in Leonardo da Vinci's manuscripts is a unique feeling, many of his riddles are still far from being solved."

He stops reading.

"...Discovering the countless mysteries that are still hidden in Leonardo da Vinci's manuscripts..." he repeats.

"Revealing the secrets of the manuscripts?" he asks himself ambitiously.

Leo's thoughts focus on a single memory.

"The visit to the museum!" he exclaims with a smile.

Many years before he had visited the National Museum of Science and Technology in Milan with his dear grandfather, a day he would never forget.

A wing of the museum was devoted to many of Leonardo's greatest inventions that only modern-day technology has allowed us to build and to discover that everything works as predicted.

In fact, many recent developments relate to notes described by the prodigious da Vinci in his manuscripts, leaving speechless those who for years had the solution to their problems to hand without ever finding it.

"Recognizing in the manuscripts an invention by my master?" he asks himself doubtfully.

Overwhelmed by such a prospect he sets the book down on the pillow and crawls under the duvet.

*** *** ***

The intrinsic difficulties in the manuscripts are significant.

In addition to the complexity of deciphering the writing there is an evident complication in decoding information that Leonardo da Vinci deliberately concealed.

From his earliest works he exercised his imagination in an innovative fashion by setting down his thoughts on paper.

He scribbled furiously, evaluating various alternatives.

He would pass from one side to the other of the sheet, filling it with ideas; some suggested to him almost by chance by his own always rather confused scribbles.

He sometimes restricted himself to writing a few lines in his notebooks in the form of a quiz, of a mysterious note, subsequently using them as a pastime with friends and students.

In; Felice (felce); Setaccio; Perla; More;

"Infelice se taccio per l'amore"

(Unhappy if I keep silent for love)

The great genius was not only a precursor of modern technology, but also a subtle humorist.

Leo's mission becomes more and more complex; the obstacles on his path are numerous. Not least of which is the fact that it is believed that Leonardo's remarkable mirror writing was the expedient of a brilliant man eager to make his writings more obscure.

*** *** ***

The rebuses were one of Leonardo da Vinci's passions; many of them have only recently been interpreted: countless sequences of words scattered across different pages.

He enjoyed himself in this way with his students.

There are also those however who think that it was a way of hiding his inventions.

Several letters, words or images are set down in such a way as to form one or more groups that, when translated, give rise to words or sentences.

The game consists in translating into words the associations of letters, signs and figures, taking into account the relationships between the individual elements.

Reasoning, planning and mental gymnastics.

Leo re-reads the paragraph and memorizes the definition:

"... Successions of words, elements and drawings appear on pages perhaps devoted to other matters."

It is all becoming extremely complex, but at the same time intriguing and mysterious.

"Mission impossible!" he exclaims impulsively, taking into account that of the whole the genius's work, more than nine thousand pages of notes still exist, about a fifth of his true output. Furthermore, those pages are written in his unmistakable mirror writing, running from right to left.

Is the mission to compose and decipher a rebus hidden for centuries in a collection of nine thousand folios?

He looks the alarm clock on the bedside table disconsolately, it is very late, his master has disappointed him this time.

In a gesture of irritation, he takes the book and throws it away, as if he wants to forget its very existence.

It is clear that the mission he has undertaken is impracticable; Thousands of pages to be deciphered to find a rebus?

He angrily switches off the light and gives himself up to a deep sleep.

Chapter Six

First rebus

"*Imagination is more important than knowledge.*"

Albert Einstein, 1879-1955, German physicist

The fever has dropped.

Lying on the bed, Leonardo observes in the semi-darkness the poster of the Ideal Man.

As usual, he cannot just glance at the drawing, he observes it, studies the details, analyzes.

The old alarm clock says 22:41.

The rain is pouring down and the balcony rain seems to be punctuating the seconds.

"Why not?" he exclaims, breaking the silence.

He jumps out of bed and picks up his grandfather's old book again, aware that the solution might be found among those pages, albeit hidden with complex stratagems.

He starts reading again from where he left off.

"The Passion for Rebuses!" the short chapter is entitled.

Intrigued by this, Leo continues to examine the sentence, summarizing its basic concepts.

"He amused himself mentally, he hid numerous rebuses in his manuscripts and some of them have only recently been discovered and interpreted."

He raises his eyes to heaven and silence reigns in the bedroom.

He returns to the text and tries to concentrate on the words, proceeding by logical steps.

"The genius's mind concealed a number of mysteries in the form of rebuses within his notes."

He sighs and continues reading.

"They are words, thoughts or drawings scattered across several pages, apparently without any connections between them."

For Leonardo da Vinci it was a simple game through which he enjoyed stimulating his students' minds.

The paragraph underlines his great skill in this exercise, leading to an expression for mystery that nowadays has become common usage: the famous Leonardesque style.

What if this was actually the beginning of the journey?

*** *** ***

Leo gets out of bed and after having found his slippers he goes hungrily toward the kitchen where he eats before going back upstairs to his bedroom.

He finds the book waiting for him, open where he had left it, once again ready to accompany him on his long journey.

Turning down the blankets, he continues with his reading and analyses.

What particularly excites his curiosity is his awareness of the existence of unsolved mysteries hidden in the manuscripts, which could only be reconstructed and deciphered through the reasoning of a mind as lively as that of his master.

From that moment Leon decides to take a different approach to his reading.

He opts for an analysis of the text in the Leonardesque style, following up what he considers to be crucial details and ignoring the numbering of the pages.

After having examined the paragraph again, trusting his decision to try to get closer to the master's style, he decides to proceed logically, following the messages dictated by the text.

"Manuscripts full of rebuses!" he confirms, summarizing the words reported in the paragraph.

"Kept in Windsor!" he confirms as he continues reading.

His mind freezes.

He closes the book and throws it on the bed without even memorizing the page number as it is no longer of any importance.

His slippers are now well placed beside the bed.

In a flash he rushes downstairs to the living room, turns on the light and sits in front the computer.

He connects to the Internet and types the address of the online encyclopaedia.

In the search box he writes: "Windsor".

The result is immediate and extremely detailed.

He starts carefully reading.

Windsor Castle, situated in the English county of Berkshire close to London, dates back to the age of William the Conqueror.

Together with Buckingham Palace in London, it is one of the British monarchy's main official residences.

Intrigued by the description, our student explores further by using a search engine.

Among the many pages devoted to the topic, he chooses one of the first on the list.

Leo attentively reads the presentation.

"In the 1930s, the celebrated Duke of Windsor became famous for having launched a fashion: a large and perfectly symmetrical tie knot."

Actually the Windsor knot is the most famous and one of the most widely used knots in the world, despite being difficult to tie.

It is without doubt the most attractive and complete.

The descriptions are numerous, but in the end they all agree that when we speak of a Windsor we are talking about the most famous of tie knots.

Leo is a lover of ties; he has around a hundred ties of various kinds and colours.

He leans back from the computer screen with a thoughtful air.

"Two eras so far apart!" he muses with a detached tone.

"Five centuries!" he murmurs disconsolately.

Will he find a link between Leonardo da Vinci and the Duke of Windsor?

He approaches the keyboard again and, observing the list of the results proposed by the search engine, he decides to investigate the details of the Duke's life.

An interesting and exhaustive page devoted to him confirms:

"The Duke of Windsor became famous for having launched a fashion for a large knot..."

Leo's first thought is that in his master's time neither ties nor anything similar existed.

However he then remembers that he has read in certain studies devoted to Leonardo da Vinci, that certain leading scholars believe that had he existed in our time, he would have surely worn a tie, for a simple matter of image, style and authority.

Da Vinci loved to stand out, he wanted to be different and to present a very particular and original image of himself and his thinking.

His commitment to the physical appearance leads us to believe that the master might be even have been a stylist.

Considering his facility in drawing combined with his boundless creativity, the "da Vinci as stylist" hypothesis is perfectly plausible.

Supporting such a supposition there are his prophetic powers that would have allowed him to anticipate and to foresee fashions.

The American artist Andy Warhol lends weight to this theory when speaking of Leonardo in the same breath as the great stylists of today: "... no artist can be compared to such a genius, today the new Leonardos are Armani and the other Italian stylists."

He turns off the computer and goes upstairs to his bedroom.

"A stylist. Could Leonardo have been a stylist?" he asks himself.

His bedroom is lit by the usual red glow.

He retrieves the book from among the blankets and lies down.

Considering the details he has discovered, he decides to focus on his research.

He goes back to the end of the book and scrolls down the list of chapters.

After a few seconds, his finger stops on a page.

"Interesting!" he says, in a somewhat surprised tone.

Page 23 is entitled: "Leonardo in Milan."

This was the first of many stages of his new life away from Florence, so the book tells, emphasising that he was sent to Milan by Lorenzo de' Medici, the famous Lorenzo il Magnifico, to work at the court of the Duke Ludovico Sforza, known as il Moro.

The book recalls that it was actually in the capital of fashion that Leonardo painted some of his most famous works such as The Virgin of the Rocks and the Last Supper.

Our student stops and reflects upon the lines he has just read.

"The capital of fashion!" he bursts out.

He goes back to the paragraph devoted to the matter and goes over it more carefully in search of who knows what detail.

Many words underlined by the authors of the book highlight their importance, but these sometimes distract the reader's attention and lead him to miss other points.

Around halfway down the page he found the key he was looking for.

"He designs new costumes!" he reads aloud.

"My master really was a stylist!" exclaims Leo, proudly confirming the great Andy Warhol's quotation.

Even though it is past midnight, Leo does not feel tired.

He is completely absorbed in his research, and another sleepless night looms.

*** *** ***

With the book and his notebook in his hand he returns to the computer.

After the usual waiting for the machine to boot up, he goes back to the search engine.

"Leonardo da Vinci in Milan" he types in the search field.

The phrase brings up a remarkable number of hits.

Many links are expressly dedicated to da Vinci's important sojourn in Milan.

After a quick glance at the list, nothing particularly catches his eye or at least nothing that would appear to bring him back on track.

He therefore decides to look at the first page.

"Sforza Castle" the home page announces in big block capitals.

"Sforza Castle is, along with the Cathedral, the most imposing monument in Milan, founded by Galeazzo II Visconti and rebuilt by Francesco Sforza in 1450."

Leo raises his eyes from the monitor and says to himself, "My master went to Milan to work at the court of Duke Francesco Sforza!"

Intrigued, he continues reading.

"It was Ludovico il Moro who called to court great artists to decorate the Castle, among whom were Donato Bramante and Leonardo da Vinci, who introduced himself as a military and civil engineer and only subsequently as a sculptor and a painter."

"A military and civil engineer too!" Leo laughs.

He continues reading.

"Leonardo's most famous creation in the Castle is the large fresco on the ceiling of the "Sala delle Asse." Here the great artist painted a false pergola, intertwining branches of sixteen trees that constitute the Vincian emblem."

"Wow, hit and sunk!" he shouts victoriously.

*** *** ***

The question that he had asked himself shortly before, about whether there could be a connection between Leonardo da Vinci and the Duke of Windsor, was now answered.

"The celebrated Duke of Windsor is still today remembered for his knot" the student remembers and proceeds with the reasoning.

"The da Vinci emblem is a system of knots."

With an air of determination he goes back to the search engine and types:

"Leonardo da Vinci + knots"

The Renaissance genius's devotion to knots is well documented.

Numerous works bear witness to this passion, from the aforementioned fresco in Milan's Sforza Castle through to the famous "Design of Knots" at the British Museum in London.

Leo is motionless, absorbed by myriad thoughts.

His mind is considering the several coincidences, trying to link them to one another.

"Could Leonardo da Vinci have invented a tie knot like the Duke of Windsor did?" he wonders with a smile.

His imagination crystallises.

"He was a prophet and a stylist!" he confirms as he came down to earth.

"Why couldn't he have done?"

He leaves the computer and returns to the index in his book.

He continues from where he left off, as ever keen to keep a grip on the logical sequence of events.

One of the topics that followed on page 36 was titled "Life at court."

Attracted by what his master's life at court might have been like he turns to that page.

The great man actually enjoyed an intensive life at court, which was where he developed his "three-quarter portrait".

On the following page there actually is a reproduction of the beautiful Lucrezia Crivelli, then the Duke Ludovico il Moro's mistress.

"Heh, heh!" giggles Leo, imagining the shady goings-on at court, but his laughter is soon cut short.

A thought pierces his mind and the once again a shiver runs down his spine.

He half-closes the book with decision, almost as if he wanted to interrupt that sensation.

Within a few seconds the tension on his face turns into a deep smile.

He rests his shoulders against the wall after having rearranged the pillow.

"Well!" he exclaims.

"It's hardly possible that it could be so simple!" he thinks incredulously.

He casts a glance at the cover of the book and, raising his eyes heavenwards, he comments, "So Granddad, this is where the story gets complicated!"

Then, with the same intensity, he observes Leonardo Da Vinci's self-portrait and laughs "Well, you are known as the genius, after all."

These exchanges with his master are increasingly frequent, creating a surreal relationship between the two minds.

He returns to page and the portrait of Il Moro's mistress.

Leo now pronounces what he had previously only been able to surmise.

"Leonardo's clothes anticipate fashions!"

The short chapter, with the exception of the interesting quotation about the Duke's mistress, does much other useful information.

Towards the end, however, a short passage attracts his attention: "...thanks to the picture it was the fashion, at the beginning of the 19th century, to wear a ribbon on the forehead..."

In a work such as this Leonardo the prophet was ahead of his time by at least three centuries.

In short, he did what today the majority of established stylists try to do, anticipate the times and impose fashions.

Supporting this ability was a determination to succeed in distinguishing himself and to express himself through an original, avant-garde personality.

Extremely unconventional, Leonardo was already considered a master of style in his own era.

Time: 01:34. Leonardo leaves the computer and moves over to the bed, he puts the book on the bedside table, the notebook above the alarm clock and he turns off the light.

He tries to relax in his usual way by summarizing the day and recalling the highlights.

His thoughts naturally turn to his book, a new companion of adventure, to the possible meaning of those pages and to those so typically Leonardesque parallels.

The only certainty is that the Master loved rebuses, and wrote lines and lines of words and drawings on diverse pages, apparently without meaning.

For the moment he has found a number of correlated details.

There was no sleeping that evening, too many thoughts were running through his head. He turns on the light and reaches out his hand toward the notebook.

The moment before falling asleep has always been the most fertile for Leo, that gives form to his ideas and inspirations with paper and pen.

He makes notes and sketches that on the following days only he can decipher.

This custom connects him to Da Vinci who also worked in the same way, as described by Giorgio Vasari:

"He tries his thoughts on the paper, scribbling furiously, considering the several alternatives and running from one side to the other of the sheet, filling it with ideas, some suggested - almost by accident - by his own marks, always rather confused."

Leo is accustomed to pronouncing his thoughts in a whisper as they materialize in notes:

"Leonardo da Vinci loved rebuses!" he states as a basis for his argument.

"The rebuses are kept in Windsor Castle", he continues in a low voice.

"Windsor Castle, where the Duke of the same name invented the most famous tie knot in the world, thus changing fashion."

He closes his eyes to summarize it all in his mind.

He sighs and continues.

"Fashion imposed by the prophet da Vinci just like by the great stylists of today."

Motionless, he mentally runs through the several passages once again.

With his left hand he directs the beam of the lamp carefully towards the notebook.

"So!" he exclaims, as if in an attempt to gather his thoughts.

At that moment he remembers a passage in the book in which it is stated that the genius had hidden a number of mysteries disguised as rebuses within his own notes.

"So why not try to decipher them?" he thinks.

He grasps his pen and decides to summarize the sentences that he has mentally assembled with a single keyword.

"Leonardo Da Vinci loved rebuses."

He stresses and writes in the notebook the crucial word: "Rebuses"

The second step is "Rebuses kept in Windsor Castle."

He notes the second element: "Windsor"

He quickly continues with his summary:

"Windsor Castle where the Duke invented the most famous tie knot in the world, thus changing fashion."

In his usual clumsy handwriting he scribbles the third keyword: "Fashion"

He raises his eyes for a moment and, after having encountered the gaze of da Vinci's self-portrait on the cover of the book, he concentrates once again.

He energetically summarizes the last sentence.

"Fashion imposed by the prophet da Vinci just like by the great stylists of today."

He extrapolates the fundamental link.

"Stylists"

Leo smiles and proceed despite finding all this highly unusual.

Rebuses

Windsor

Fashion

Stylists

His notebook now contains four keywords.

With a smile still on his lips, he continues to stare at his notes.

The master has set his new student a test.

Leonardo da Vinci hid these words to test his own students' qualities, most probably to evaluate those who were capable of approaching his own way of thinking and his imagination.

Right now, however, it has become a personalized rebus.

His mind considers those four clues over and over again, aware that this might be the first rebus that the master has expressly created for him.

The rain increases, the tinkling on the railing starting to become intrusive.

The wind rattles the shutters.

It is a strange night, certainly sleepless for anyone unable to find the solution to those words.

In Leonardo's mind the thought becomes as incessant as the rain.

What is the connection between those four keys?

What is the solution to the rebus?

He picks up his scribbled notes again and after some minutes a triumphant smile crosses his face.

"Discovering consists in seeing what everybody has seen and in thinking what nobody has thought" he comments plucking up courage.

He returns to the page where the four crucial words are listed and he begins to correlate them with rapid associations:

"The Windsor knot imposed a fashion"

"Stylists use the Windsor knot to impose a fashion"

"The rebus of the knot is used by the stylists"

Leonardo stops his fast reasoning and raises his eyes to heaven.

"Elementary!" he exclaims with an air of jubilation.

"The rebus of the Windsor knot dictates fashion for the stylists" he states firmly.

With a satisfied air he observes the solution of the rebus.

Is this his mission? Is this the work that Leonardo Da Vinci has commissioned from him?

Proudly he turns over the pages of the notebook and stops at the page where he had initially drawn up the two columns about the commissioned works.

He neatly sums up the solution of the rebus and he inserts it into the empty cell:

"Rebus of the tie knot"

Confraternity	Leonardo Da Vinci
Leonardo Da Vinci	Leo
8 december 1484	8 december 2008
virgin of the rocks	rebus of the tie knot

The mission is clear: to decipher one of the most common dilemmas faced by all men and even some women at least once in their lives: how to knot a tie.

"The rebus of the tie knot!" he repeats with satisfaction and curiosity.

This is the mission the Renaissance genius has asked him to complete within the year 2008.

Now everything is clear.

By adopting Leonardesque reasoning he has constructed and deciphered the first rebus.

But how many are there waiting to be discovered and to be revealed?

*** *** ***

Deep silence envelopes the room, the rain subsides suddenly and the shutters are still.

It is as if the surrounding environment reflects his mood, now peaceful and satisfied.

That night he feels that he is a little closer to his master.

He puts his precious notebook on the bedside table next to the alarm clock reading 2:14.

The bedroom is now dark, with only the glow of the streetlamp penetrating the gaps in the shutters illuminating the poster of the Vitruvian Man.

Leo is proud of his discovery; he now knows his mission.

He puts his head on the pillow and abandons himself to deep sleep.

The solution of the first rebus leaves no room for interpretation.

It is clear and leads to one of the most common dilemmas in the real life of a man: how to knot a tie.

Had the genius of Leonardo da Vinci really been turned to this matter too?

Is the solution of to the problem hidden in his notes?

Chapter Seven

Second Rebus

"... then those enigmas predestined to seduction emerge..."

Friedrich Nietzsche, 1844-1900, German philosopher and writer

It is a lovely Sunday morning, the month of March bringing a little warm weather, the temperature pleasant despite the snow still covering the ground.

Leo wakens to bells replacing the buzzer of his old alarm clock.

The church of the small village is not far from his house, and the ringing announcing the start of Mass can hardly be ignored.

Cold water is an excellent antidote for a rude awakening.

He refreshes himself by running his big hands full of water through his long hair.

He raises the shutters and goes out onto the balcony for a few minutes to watch as the square begins to become crowded. Re-entering, he half-closes the door and he throws himself back onto the still unmade bed.

Motivated by the discovery of the first rebus he decides to start reading again, looking for something, maybe the composition of a second rebus, with other details or connections hidden in who knows which corner of the book or Internet pages.

His grandfather's book is on the bedside table. Inside it is his notebook.

He is sure that if the Renaissance genius had led him to that solution he would have something else to offer.

The master would not have disappointed him, but without doubt the task ahead of him would be anything but simple.

Trusting in his own Leonardesque style, he would have concealed the other keywords in his manuscripts: all that Leo has to do is find them and decipher them.

"Where should I start?" he wonders wryly.

The thousands of pages of notes written by the da Vinci are crammed with indications: it is like looking for a needle in a haystack.

In the index at the end of the book he finds a chapter dedicated to this immense and priceless inheritance, with the title "Endless sheets of notes."

Leonardo is hardly hopeful, but, on the other hand, he has to start somewhere.

Browsing through the pages quickly he reaches page 84 where the matter is dealt with.

The difficulty in that period of finding paper to write on is underlined.

It was a precious commodity and was therefore exploited to the full. In addition, the chapter also stressed the master's habit of writing down everything that passed through his mind for the fear of losing his own ideas.

Unfortunately, proceeding in this way and having to use the paper sparingly, his notes are very confused. Able to deal with a certain number of topics on one page, they are sometimes radically different from one another and even written at different times.

On page 85 there is an interesting and exhaustive chart that summarizes the places where the majority of Leonardo da

Vinci's manuscripts are kept, scattered throughout the world in castles, libraries, museums and art galleries. The now familiar Windsor Castle immediately catches Leo's attention.

In London, in addition to the Royal Library at Windsor Castle where the anatomical manuscripts are kept, we find other very famous codexes in the library of the Victoria and Albert Museum: the Forster Codes.

Leo has visited London several times but only due to work commitments, without ever having had the time for cultural visits.

"What a pity!" he exclaims with an irritated gesture.

Our student decides therefore to investigate with the help of the computer. Going to the online encyclopaedia he types "Victoria and Albert Museum London." A detailed description appears on the monitor: "The Victoria and Albert Museum is situated on Cromwell Road in London. It is the most important museum in the world dedicated to the applied arts and lesser arts, although there are also sections devoted to painting, sculpture and architecture."

Leo stops and raises his eyes to heaven, after a few moments he exclaims:

"Impossible!"

He cannot believe his own eyes; it cannot be that the Master granted him such a gift, a crucial clue, without complicating his life.

"Victoria and Albert!" he repeats with a sure tone.

Leo is sure of the meaning hidden in those two names but he wants further confirmation. He connects to the homepage of the search engine, by now stored among his favourites.

"Victoria and Albert" he types again and with a click he starts the search.

"Et voilà!" he exclaims in satisfaction. "Another two tie knots!" he states proudly.

Victoria and Albert are actually two names for tie knots, less famous than the Windsor, but still well known.

The Victoria knot is similar to the Four-in-Hand in appearance, but it is bigger and is very useful when the tie that you are using is very thin or worn-out.

The Albert knot is similar to the simple knot, the only difference being that it consists of a second step, making it perfect for the Italian collar and slightly thin net ties.

"Elementary, my dear Watson!" he comments with an English aplomb recalling the successful television series dedicated to the crime stories of Sherlock Holmes.

Surprised by the ease of this discovery he decides to follow up the lead.

He types in the usual search engine: "tie knot." As ever numerous results appear. He starts to visit some of them but fails to find anything of interest.

One of the last links attracts his attention with an intriguing presentation:

"In the male symbolic iconography the knot represented union, marriage, fertility and thus life" he reads aloud.

"Fascinating!" he exclaims with amazement.

He moves the mouse and with a click he enters the site.

After a few sentences comes a description of how to knot a tie:

"With a few precise gestures it becomes as easy as lacing up your shoes. To achieve a simple knot, the most popular, it is necessary to position..."

He re-reads the sentence and comments:

"If it's called a simple knot there'll be a reason!"

He returns to the search engine and with curiosity he types:

"simple knot".

He glances through the page visualizing the first results.

His attention immediately focuses on the sixth result, presented with this sentence: "The Simple Double Knot, also known as Prince Albert, is similar to the Simple Knot."

He enters the website.

On the left, 17 ways of tying of knots appear with their respective names, from the simple knot to the complex Balthus.

Things are definitely looking up.

The connections follow one another and confirm our student's thoughts.

He picks the book up again and turns to the pages of the tome found in the attic; he does not want to lose the guideline in Leonardesque style.

He re-reads the paragraph and takes up once again the fil rouge he had left shortly before.

"The Forster I, II and III Manuscripts, kept in the library of the Victoria and Albert Museum."

Intrigued, he checks to see whether there are any pages in the book devoted to these codexes.

Unfortunately, nothing is mentioned in the index.

He leafs through the volume, sure that the author of the book will have investigated this matter.

"Damn!" he exclaims in an irritated tone.

"There is nothing about the Forster Codes" he confirms in defeat.

He picks up the book and leafs through it again.

He is aware that the story is hanging by a thread: having materialised out of nothing, it could just as easily vanish into thin air again.

The chain of coincidences is very delicate.

Should just one element be missing, everything would become meaningless.

The positive air of a few moments earlier is replaced by a sense of impotence.

Now there is a sense of stark pessimism in the atmosphere.

He closes the book and observing Leonardo Da Vinci's self-portrait on the cover he jokes as if to defuse the moment:

"Not now, genius, don't play tricks!"

This time his smile is less spontaneous.

He returns to the index and re-reads the list of chapters carefully.

Nothing.

Frustrated, he begins all over again; he leafs through the pages one by one.

"Bingo!" he exults, as if he had just completed a card at the village hall.

Page 120.

"Notes on Flight" is the title of the chapter.

On the strength of the bold words at the beginning of the paragraph begin his spirits to recover.

"The three Forster Codes" he confirms proudly.

The bitterness in his mouth turns into a sweet aftertaste.

Happy to have picked up the thread again he concentrates on reading.

Three paper manuscripts, bound in parchment with the particularity of being pocketsize and known as Forster I, Forster II and Forster III.

They passed to Earl Lytton before being inherited by John Forster, from whom they clearly derive their names.

In 1876, Forster left them to the museum where they are still conserved.

They contain studies of geometry, weights and hydraulic machines developed by the da Vinci between 1493 and 1505.

It would seem that the master used such notebooks of various forms for occasional writings. For this reason they were pocketsize: handy for taking notes on the spur of the moment.

"Just like my notebook!" Leo exclaims, glancing at his precious notebook.

These codexes focus in particular on Leonardo Da Vinci's studies of geometry, a subject of particular interest to him.

Confirming this, the book features his research into an enigma that has intrigued many mathematicians for centuries.

He immediately finds the reference in the index at page 130:

"The squaring of the circle".

Since ancient times, this has been one of the most closely analysed issues in geometry. It consists of creating, with the aid of only ruler and compass, a square whose area is equal to the given circle.

In Leo's fingers the pages now flicked through faster, more confidently and more directly.

The paragraph describes the master's passion for geometry.

The many studies in his manuscripts confirm it, particularly all the sketches and notes concerning polyhedrons, considered to be the basis of cosmogonist theories in which the dodecahedron is considered by Plato to be the image of the universe in its totality.

In the Italian Renaissance regular polyhedrons were excellent subjects for perspective studies.

Besides Leonardo da Vinci, many other celebrities of the past ventured into this field .

"Interesting!" comments Leo, also a lover of geometry.

On the same page he notices some pencil sketches made by the da Vinci.

They are all geometric sketches, in particular a hexagon, probably used as a starting point.

"And what are these?" he wonders intrigued.

"Symbols?"

Leonardo pays attention to the details that for many might be of little significance.

The hexagonal figure features a number of curious symbols at its points.

They seem to indicate steps of some kind.

"Numbers perhaps?" our student wonders as he stares at the drawing.

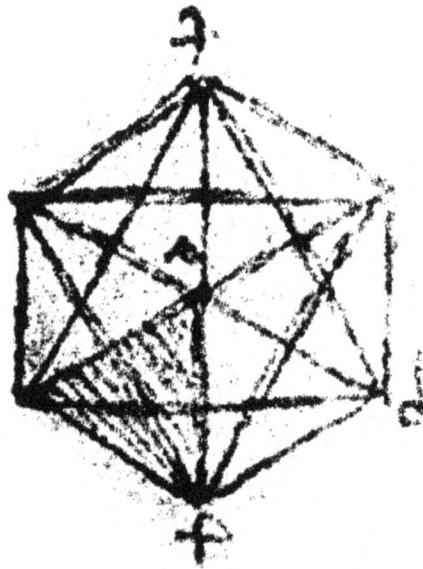

Da Vinci seems to denominate every point with a symbol, perhaps indicating a position, numbering them perhaps to remember their sequence.

Aware that when you set about studying the master's work you can neglect nothing, Leo decides to investigate that hexagon.

The symbol that mostly attracts his attention is below the lowest point.

"Indecipherable!" he confirms looking at it closely.

Intrigued, he nonetheless decides to get closer to somehow grasping its meaning.

From the box where he keeps the objects that his grandfather left him he fishes out an old magnifying glass; used by the old man in the last years of his life to read the newspapers.

He brings the glass closer to the page and, moving very carefully, he tries to focus on the image.

Despite the magnification, the symbol remains indecipherable.

He places the glass carefully on the pillow.

What can its meaning be?

What was the genius indicating out with that scribble?

He picks up the magnifying glass again and returns to the book.

Leonardo's eyes light up.

"Brilliant!" he exclaims.

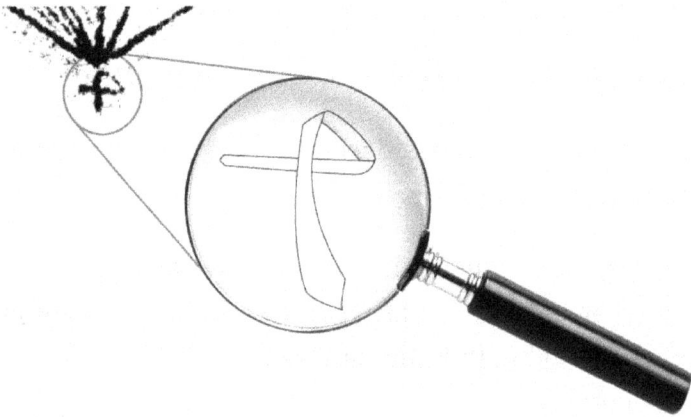

"Incredibly brilliant!" he repeats.

In the light of the clues found up to that moment, this last symbol seemingly without meaning also finds its own significance.

"A step in the knotting of a tie!" he confirms proudly.

With this clue the Renaissance genius had illustrated a precise step in the realization of a knot.

*** *** ***

Late that evening he comes back home, after having had dinner with friends.

Wasting no time, he goes upstairs to his bedroom, gets undressed for bed and picks up his beloved notebook; he has to summarize what the genius has reserved for him through those last details, looking for a second rebus to be composed and then deciphered.

After the successful experience of the first rebus he decides to use the same system.

Four keywords, hidden in the various paragraphs.

He lies back on the pillow and begins a reconstruction of the steps found so far.

"Victoria and Albert Museum", Leo affirms with certainty.

Two other names of tie knots.

He is aware that this could be the first clue of the second rebus and therefore attaches a lot of importance to it.

He proceeds logically.

"With the Windsor knot being the most famous, why should I consider two others that are little known?" he wonders.

With an aura of perplexity he grasps his pen and a little dubiously air writes "Simple knot", recalling the old grandfather's words, who often told him to cross where water is shallow when he was not sure of the path to follow.

He observes the first keyword and continues.

"The Forster Codes are preserved in this museum!" our student exclaims.

"Three pocketsize manuscripts!" he continues logically.

"Mostly full of geometric studies."

He stops and picks up the book again, open at the page with the hexagon.

He observes the geometric figure again and muses out loud:

"A hexagon with the symbol of a step in knotting a tie at the base."

He is sure that the creation of the second rebus passes by way of that important discovery.

Just a single keyword figures in his notebook so far.

As usual Leo summarizes the information in the interests of clarity.

He decides to enter the details in two columns.

In the first cell he writes:

"Victoria and Albert".

In the adjacent one he enters the first keyword:

"Simple knot"

He goes over the second sentence again in his head:

"The Forster Codes are preserved in this museum."

Proceeding logically he writes in the second line logic:

"Forster Codes".

After a moment's thought, he recalls the shape of the codexes and, confidently writes in the next box:

"Pocketsize".

He raises his eyes as if searching for further inspiration.

He sighs and starts again always using the same technique.

"Codexes full of geometric studies" he affirms.

As a reference to this detail he indicates the keyword, the geometric figure at the base of the Master's studies:

"Hexagon"

Continuing to fill in the table he reaches the last of the four lines.

Two cells remain empty.

"The hexagon with the symbol of a step in knotting a tie."

Increasingly convinced about the definition, he also fills in the last empty space: "Steps"

He gets his breath back with a depth sigh.

Having already tackled the problem once and aware of the procedure, Leo immediately moves on to the search for the second rebus.

Its construction surely lies with those keywords.

He tears the sheet out his notebook and, holding it in his left hand, he recopies the crucial words.

simple knot

pocket-size

hexagon

steps

Leonardo dwells on the four elements.

After some minutes he gets up, leaving the book on the pillow.

He goes downstairs to the kitchen and gets something to drink from the fridge.

Those clues are echoing in his mind.

The computer was still displaying the page dealing with the simple knot.

He casts a glance at the steps proposed with some simple sketches for the execution of the knot and, miming the movements, he approaches the monitor.

He remembers that many years before, during his army recruiting school, he was the only one in his section to know how to knot a tie.

On their few evenings off, the elegant uniform provided by the army was obligatory, tie included.

Having knotted their tie once some of his fellow soldiers kept that same knot for the entire four-month training period.

Smiling at these memories, he turns off the computer.

He goes back upstairs to his bedroom.

On the pillow he finds his notebook with its four keywords:

"Simple knot - Pocketsize - Hexagon - Steps"

The second rebus is surely linked to the first, he thinks.

He flicks through the pages of the notebook, looking for the first rebus.

He tears out the page where he noted the clues to the first rebus and at the bottom of the page dedicated to the second, he copies the keywords:

"Rebus - Windsor - Fashion - Stylists"

He raises his eyes and adjusting the beam of light from the lamp, he writes down the solution:

"The rebus of the tie knot."

He stops for a second and returns to the four words:

"Simple knot - Pocketsize - Hexagon - Steps"

Leo is having trouble this time.

He tries various possible combinations over and over again with no result.

His mind is focused on the elements that might lead him to the solution of the second rebus.

"The master asks me to decipher the mystery of the tie knot" he states confidently.

"Now, is he going to tell me how to do it?" he wonders not quite so confidently.

*** *** ***

"From right to left!" he exclaims in triumph.

Actually anyone intending to study Leonardo da Vinci should be aware that among his myriad peculiarities was his gift for mirror writing.

The solution to the second enigma is to be read as follows:

"Steps on a pocketsize hexagon for a simple knot."

The genius points out that to complete a simple tie knot, steps effected on a hexagonal pocketsize object are required.

"Brilliant!"

Leonardo takes a blank sheet from the notebook and summarizes the first two rebuses with their solutions.

First Rebus

REBUS - WINDSOR - FASHION - STYLISTS

Solution: The rebus of the tie knot

Second Rebus

SIMPLE KNOT - POCKETSIZE - HEXAGON - STEPS

Solution: Steps on a pocketsize hexagon for a simple knot

With a satisfied air he places his precious notebook on the bedside table.

He has found, reconstructed and deciphered the first two rebuses.

At that moment in Leo's thoughts there is the certainty that the work reserved for him is set.

Allowing each one to knot the tie.

Chapter Eight

Third rebus

"It is clear that Leonardo, through his comprehension of art, began many things and never finished one of them."

Giorgio Vasari, 1511-1574, Italian painter and sculptor

Was the master jealous of his inventions and his codes?

Why did not he not want to make it easy for his manuscripts to be read?

A secret language created to conceal what secret?

Once it was believed that the peculiarity of da Vinci's mirror handwriting was merely the expedient of a remarkable man eager to make his writings, and particularly his precious codexes, more secure.

The mirror writing runs from right to left, and can only be deciphered by using a mirror.

Intrigued by the enigma of the genius's handwriting, Leo goes to the pages dedicated to this peculiar trait.

The chapter dealing with the matter is found at page 185.

"… he was left-handed and wrote from right to left, often using mirror hand, he also wrote his notes from the bottom, starting from the last page…"

As already mentioned, of the whole of Leonardo da Vinci's output, about nine thousand pages of notes remain, mostly written in his unmistakable handwriting.

Leo's mission has so far seen excellent results achieved by following simple logic, but the thought of having to decipher, in addition to the rebuses, the enigmas of the great man's handwriting frighten him.

Aware of this additional difficulty, he returns stubbornly to his reading.

The bookmark takes him back to the page with the hexagon and its unusual symbols, on the basis of which he had reconstructed the second rebus.

He once again sets about exploring in search of new elements.

In block capitals he notes the title of the page.

"The squaring of the circle"

Along with the problem of trisecting the angle and that of the duplication of the cube, the squaring of the circle constitutes a classical problem of Greek geometry.

The aim is to construct, using only a ruler and compass, a square with the same area as a given circle.

Illustrious mathematicians worked on the problem for centuries, without ever managing to solve it.

The book reports that Leonardo also took up this important challenge, although even he was unable to come up with a solution.

Leo picks up his magnifying glass again.

He inspects the page is search of some other details.

With a steady hand he examines the figures drawn in the margins of the page, mostly representing geometric sketches by the master.

The curious symbols drawn at the borders of the geometric figures always prove to be indecipherable.

"They look like numbers!" our student decides.

"Elements representing numbers; an unusual form of writing" he confirms, intrigued.

Numbers originated in India and reached Europe through the work of Arab mathematicians and astronomers.

Subsequently Leonardo Fibonacci promoted the Arabic numerical system in Europe.

Leonardo da Vinci was born in 1452, on the threshold of this epochal change.

It is for this reason that in his manuscripts he uses an Arab numbering system that is nowadays incomprehensible.

After having carefully observed those strange elements, Leo stands up and, moving over to the computer, he mumbles, "the answer is surely on the Internet."

After the usual wait for the programmes to load, he connects to the essential search engine.

He pauses to think about what to search for.

After a few moments he confidently types:

"Evolution of the writing of numbers"

The usual exhaustive list of results appears in a few tenths of a second.

"A needle in the haystack!" he dispairs.

Hoping to narrow down the results he decides to turn to the online encyclopaedia.

A wise decision.

The encyclopaedia uses thumbnails that allow the Internet user to recognize immediately the utility of the page displayed.

Leonardo goes back upstairs to the bedroom, picks up his book and, going down stairs again he leafs through it to page 130.

Halfway down the stairs he stops suddenly.

He notes that in the drawings published in the book the Master frequently inserts identical signs.

His intuition that they are actually numbers is gathering strength.

He reaches the computer and puts the book next to the monitor.

He carefully scrutinises the symbols that are repeated next to the figures.

With an irritated gesture he jumps up, and running up the stairs, he returns to his bedroom to fetch the magnifying glass.

"They're identical!" he states, confirming the thought he had had shortly before.

The elements actually seem to be used by da Vinci to number the points of the geometric figures.

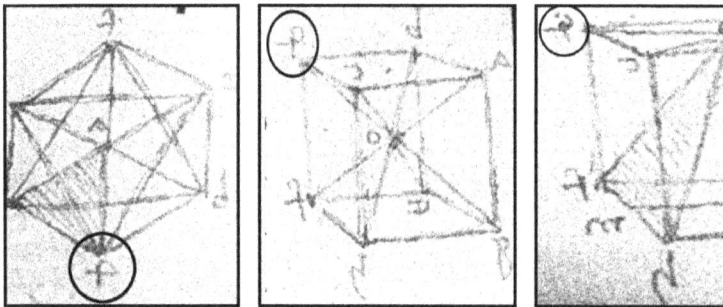

Leo starts, realising he has noticed something.

He springs up and, with the book in his right hand, he rushes into the bathroom.

The light above the mirror illuminates his face.

He reopens the book at the page in question.

His gaze is determined and he is aware of being just one step away from a crucial discovery.

He places the magnifying glass in front of the symbol that had led him to recognise the step in the knotting of a tie.

He lifts the book and reflects the page in the mirror.

A smile of wonder illuminates his face.

He takes the book again and goes over the movements very slowly.

"The number four!"

He repeats confidently.

"It's a four!" he says, looking at himself in the mirror.

The writing, deciphered with the help of a looking glass, has revealed the true meaning of those symbols.

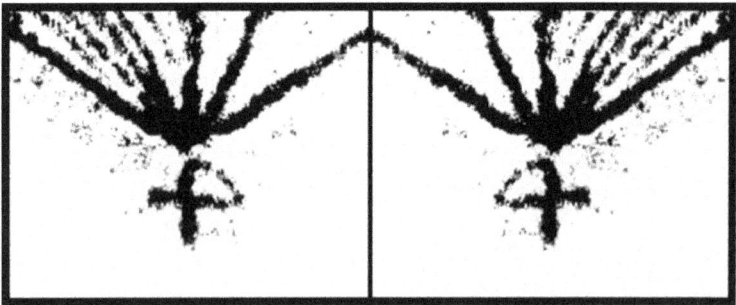

Leonardo da Vinci wrote a series of numbers beside the geometric figure, most probably to define a sequence to be followed, a numbering of steps, and all this in his mysterious mirror writing.

Proud of his discovery Leo returns to the computer.

The screen still displays the result of the search on the evolution of the numbers.

On the page there are ten numbers, from zero to nine.

Each is accompanied by a link to a descriptive page.

The choice is now obvious; he shifts with the mouse to the number four and clicks.

An interesting and exhaustive description about the development of this figure over the centuries appears.

Leo diligently saves the precious information, well aware that it will certainly be of fundamental importance in the resolution of the rebuses.

Next to the text there is a sequence of seven symbols that ends with the number four.

"Wow!" he exclaims as he looks at them.

Legend has it that this deals with the evolution of the number four from the Indians to the Europeans.

$$+ \quad \mp \quad \not{F} \quad \mathfrak{H} \quad \mathcal{F} \quad \mathcal{L} \quad \mathcal{R} \quad 4$$

"Eureka!" he cries joyfully observing the sixth element.

*** *** ***

After having eaten, our student returns to the page that has so far provided him with such satisfaction.

The paragraph below the hexagon is entitled:

"Complex Calculations"

The paragraph once gain underlines da Vinci's passion for arithmetic and mathematical calculations:

"They are tables full of complex calculations, it seems they were used for designing" he reads attentively, his curiosity aroused.

"Useful calculations for design!" he repeats.

Overwhelmed by the information he decides to sort out his thoughts in order not to overlook crucial details.

He draws a line on the notebook as if he wants to separate his new notes.

He draws four small squares in the middle of the page and in an almost illegible handwriting, he entitles the diagram:

"Third Rebus"

He looks away from the notebook and gazing at the ceiling, he reflects on the possible key passages in forming the enigma.

After some minutes of reflection he defines the first component:

"Backwards!" he affirms with a confident tone:

"Leonardo writes backwards, starting from the end, surely it is an element that should not be underestimated."

He picks up his the pen and summarizes the concept, noting it in the first box.

Still thinking about the master's peculiar handwriting, he says out loud to himself:

"Backwards."

This talent exploited by Da Vinci puzzles the student.

"He wrote backwards without using a mirror", he confirms, disorientated by such virtuosity.

He once again leafs through the pages of the book and his notes, analyzing the various steps in search of decisive clues and ideas.

"Elementary, Watson!" he exclaims with his usual catchphrase.

"The decoding of the number four!" he confirms, certain that this is a key element.

His eyes stare at the incomplete scheme.

"An element is missing!" he states.

The rebuses he has so far reconstructed are composed of four keywords and now that the decoding of the symbols has emphasised the importance of the number four, it cannot be otherwise.

He falls back on logical, elementary reasoning.

He returns to the two previous rebuses and analyzes their respective solutions, convinced of the existence of a logical thread between them, a sort of evolution: a perfect Leonardesque style stratagem.

The first rebus revealed mission to him: to develop the tie knot.

The second rebus shows him the object on which to perform the steps: a pocketsize hexagon.

Actually the notes concerning the second solution reveal the various steps for the execution of the tie knot.

The solution is a logical consequence of the second rebus.

"How to design the knot?" the student asks himself.

The third rebus should show him how to actually tie the knot.

One detail mentioned in the book catches his attention.

"Useful for the design" he states, recalling the paragraph of the book dedicated to the complicated calculations.

He goes back to the page of the notebook with the still incomplete diagram.

Writing neatly, he fills in the empty cell with the last keyword.

The next step consists in defining the solution of the rebus through a logical sentence summarizing the four elements.

He stops to contemplate his creation.

backwards

without mirror

four

for planning

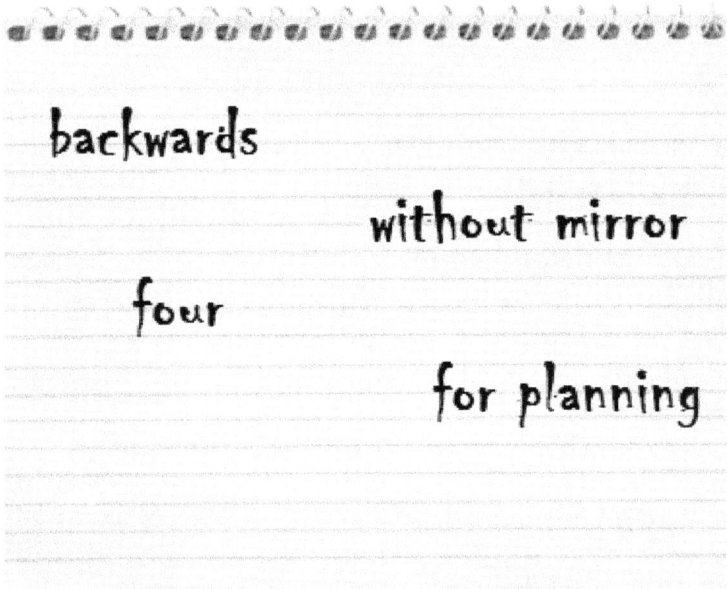

On the strength of his past experience he knows the solution is close.

"For the design four mirror steps with no mirror", he declares confidently.

*** *** ***

The student has composed and deciphered another rebus artfully concealed by his master five centuries earlier.

"Discovering consists in seeing what everybody has seen and in thinking what nobody has thought", he quotes out in satisfaction.

He tears up the scribbled sheets and chooses an empty page.

With usual care he neatly summarizes up the three rebuses and their respective solutions.

First Rebus

REBUS - WINDSOR - FASHION - STYLISTS

Solution: Rebus of the tie knot

Second Rebus

SIMPLE KNOT - POCKETSIZE - HEXAGON - STEPS

Solution: Steps on a pocketsize hexagon for a simple knot

Third Rebus

BACKWARDS - WITHOUT MIRROR - FOUR - FOR THE DESIGN

Solution: For the design four backwards steps with no mirror

Lying on the bed, he gazes at the ceiling.

He cannot keep the smile from the lips now that he has relaxed, pleased with the results he has achieved.

He has already deciphered three rebuses that he never knew existed, up to a few days before.

But how many rebuses are there still to be found among the master's myriad enigmatic notes?

Chapter Nine

Fourth rebus

Fourth rebus

"Surprising soul who had always turned his gaze to infinity and to what is concealed behind things."

Hippolyte Taine, 1865-1893. French philosopher and historian

The sentence appearing on page 130 echoes in our student's mind:

"A challenge that for once did not bring the desired results."

Leonardo da Vinci has a margin of error, he is not infallible.

After all those years of study on his master's life and works, this is the first time that he has read of someone suggesting that he had trouble solving a problem, especially as it concerned arithmetic, in which he excelled.

Leo's admiration for da Vinci is such that the admission of a single error by the great man smacks of profanity.

Adding insult to injury the chapter goes on to claim that this was "a complex method that da Vinci should not have liked, considering that out of nine attempts he found the exact result only twice. "

Leo re-reads the note three times, to be sure of what he has taken on board.

Surprised almost to the point of irritation, he decides to dwell on that passage.

"There must be a message behind such a statement. "

His admiration for his master is boundless: he considers him infallible.

Perplexed, he re-reads and stares the page.

His feeling is that this is not a simple mistake, but a message: the genius never makes a mistake and should he appear to make one it can only be because he wants to demonstrate something.

Without straying from the question in hand, he focuses his reasoning on the world of ties knots.

The correlation is obvious, it refers to a problem that affects all of us attempting this at this age-old ritual; that is, the difficulty of knotting an impeccable tie.

Our student sighs and starts over with an extremely rational argument.

"Leonardo da Vinci recognizes a problem!" he states confidently to lay the foundations for his reasoning.

"The exact result is found two times out of nine", he declares, repeating the words of the book.

Leo's eyes gaze emptily, his mind wandering.

"Elementary, Watson!" he exclaims with a satisfied giggle.

As always the solution emerges through the simple application of logic.

The genius speaks in his own particular style and one has to adopt his way of thinking to decipher his words.

Once you have discovered the real motivations behind his statements and actions, all you need to do is to contextualize them.

The difficulties in knotting a tie are evident and widely recognized, especially if you want it tied perfectly and to the correct length.

The master recognized this difficulty and associated it with a mathematical problem.

He stated that there is an objective complication to its realization and frequently the two parameters are not met.

This difficulty is proportional to the degree of complexity of realization: the more the knot is complex the more its perfect execution will be improbable.

According to the genius, only twice out of nine times is the execution perfect: a concrete difficulty of realization that led him to start from the simplest of knots.

Leo returns to the book and observes the complex mathematical sequences.

Attentively, he analyzes the figures and, after a number of muttered comments, he half-closes the book.

He feels for his slippers under the bed and quietly goes out on to the balcony.

*** *** ***

Spring is drawing near.

The days are getting longer and the sun glitters in the old fountain.

The small square is becoming crowded, the restaurants have reopened for the new season, and the first tourists are sitting at the tables.

The region in which Leo lives is famous for its mild and sunny climate, its lakes and mountains, and is a very popular destination for short breaks.

He re-enters his bedroom and lies down on the bed.

"Which is the simplest knot?" he wonders continuing his reflection.

"Which is the one that is easiest to tie?"

He continues to construct a logical argument.

"The knot that Leonardo da Vinci wanted to create without possibility of error?"

He raises his eyes in search of the solution, gazing at the white wall of the bed room, as if he is trying to free his mind of outside influences and focus on his train of thought.

"The simple knot?" he wonders out loud.

"The four-in-hand!" he decides, recalling the results of the search on the Internet.

The four-in-hand knot, as it is known to sartorial connoisseurs, is the simplest way to knot a tie, clearly consisting of four precise steps.

"Four-in-hand!" he confirms with a good English pronunciation.

The number four, hidden behind the mysterious symbol at the base of the hexagon, forcefully makes its presence felt once again.

It is certainly an element crucial to his mission.

Da Vinci continues to guide him on his journey; he nudges Leo towards the composition of his mysterious rebuses and then leaves him free to find their solutions.

Leo finds his grandfather's book among the blankets, turns to the first pages and carefully re-reads the introduction.

"Welcome to the world of a genius: Leonardo da Vinci."

Leo smiles at those words, sure that his dear grandfather would also have read them, but could never have imagined that the book hid a number of crucial details for an incredible mission.

*** *** ***

Leo has already composed and deciphered three rebuses, all consisting of four keywords.

As before, Leonardo picks up his precious notebook and, with a steady hand, he writes down what he considers to be the first element of the fourth rebus:

"Four-in-hand knot"

Accustomed to maintaining absolute clarity of thought, he decides to rewrite the solutions of the rebuses found so far.

He leafs through the notes and scribbles in his notebook, pulls out the sheets that relate to the three rebuses and summarizes them up on a new page.

First Rebus

Rebus of the Tie Knot

Second Rebus

Steps on a pocketsize hexagon for a simple knot

Third Rebus

For the design four backwards steps with no mirror

He stops and observes the three solutions at length, looking for that coherence that led him to their composition.

He is aware that in all probability a fourth rebus is missing, the one that will allow him to complete the mission.

The solutions he has found so far are correlated amongst themselves, clearly indicating three components.

With a satisfied air Leo places his pen on the bedside table and enchanted observes the three solutions.

A prisoner of his thoughts, he sighs.

"What will the last rebus be?" he wonders insistently.

"What will it deal with?"

He takes a step back in his reasoning.

"A perfectly knotted tie has to satisfy two fundamental parameters" he recalls aloud.

"The perfection of the knot and of ties' correct length."

He picks up his notebook again and observing the summary of the first three rebuses, states, "the third rebus shows me how to overcome the problem of the perfect knot."

His big green eyes sparkle, he has found the key to the puzzle.

"The fourth rebus will show me how to solve the issue of perfect length", he declares with a mixture of satisfaction and curiosity.

He puts on his slippers and goes downstairs.

He turns on the computer, logs on to the net and begins to search for a definition of the perfect length of a knotted tie.

One of the many websites dedicated to the matter puts forward the following explanation:

"The widest part of the tie, that is, the part immediately before the tip, should rest precisely on the upper edge of the belt and the thinner end should never be longer than the wide end."

In defining a precise length, the definition establishes a fundamental rule for all those wishing to knot a perfect tie according to the rules of the good taste.

Frequently, however, even the most experienced wearer of ties runs up against this fundamental parameter and has to repeat the process from the beginning.

Leo moves away from the computer.

Another test awaits him: he has to compose and then solve the fourth rebus that will reveal how to solve this dilemma.

He goes back to his bedroom and snuggles down under the duvet, with gazing into, his thoughts focused on the next step.

A ray of sunlight catches the Vitruvian Man.

Leo glances at the perfect man and jokingly asks, "So how are we going to solve this?"

He smiles, concealing a degree of preoccupation.

He has composed and deciphered three rebuses invented by the great Renaissance genius, but he is well aware that in the absence of the fourth the exercise is futile.

"I've no idea!" he exclaims, groping for a clue.

How did Leonardo da Vinci solve this fundamental passage?

Does he define a parameter somewhere in his manuscripts?

Is there a sort of universal measure hidden in his notes?

Leo is wandering into an increasingly dense jungle.

His experience with the composition of the first rebuses brings him back to the book.

While he picks up the tome once again he jokes:

"Just think Grandad, just think!"

Casually he leafs through a few pages, hoping for inspiration.

Nothing.

He returns to his notes and re-reads them carefully.

Nothing.

He is gripped by a depressing thought.

"What if this is where it ends?" he wonders with regret.

"And what if this journey remains incomplete like some of the works by my master?"

He feels a lump in his throat.

Leo recalls at that moment that when he first came into contact with the book about da Vinci a particular situation had caught his attention and shocked him.

He opens the book at page 242.

The short chapter dedicated to the Virgin of the Rocks ends with this sentence:

"... he delivered it six years later."

The disconcerted student repeats out loud, "Six years later!"

In addition to that late delivery of the work, another puzzling case is mentioned in the book.

A creation that was destined not to be passed on to posterity, a huge bronze horse, seven metres high, that was never completed.

An unfinished work to which a troubling title is applied:

"A never seen horse!"

Leo's preoccupations suddenly become all too real.

What if one of the rebuses was also an unfinished project?

The frustration is too much to bear and Leo has tears in his eyes.

With a desolate air he places the book and his notes on the bedside table.

The alarm clock reads 18:33.

"It was nice while it lasted!" he comments mournfully.

The adventure is over; his fantastic journey has drawn to a close while remaining inconclusive.

*** *** ***

Dinner was delicious; Leo's mother Sophie is an excellent cook.

The evening flows with a calm, relaxed atmosphere, with a game of cards and quiet chatter.

It is late and after having taken his leave of his loved ones Leo goes back home.

He lowers the shutters and settles down under the duvet.

"I can't believe it!" he comments a little angrily.

"It's not possible that my master has been making fun of me!"

Leo cannot fall asleep, upset by the perceived defeat.

With an irritated gesture he turns on the light and reaches out his hand toward the book.

Yet again he turn to the index.

After brief consideration he decides to look for a clue that will allow him to get closer to the matter of the fourth rebus dealing with the dilemma of perfect length.

"The Perfection of the Human Body", he exclaims as his finger runs down the list of chapter titles.

In a flash he turns to page 352.

Numerous manuscripts by da Vinci are devoted to studies of anatomy.

All the parts of the human body were analyzed by the artist, sometimes with the most macabre methods, dissecting dead bodies like a true pathologist.

Along with a humorous study of the different types of noses, the short chapter emphasizes the important studies conducted by the master and collected in the famous Treatise on the Universal Measurements of Bodies.

A significant sentence is indicated in the text:

"... In the length of the figures the universal measurements are hidden."

This is Leonardo da Vinci's universal theory, developed after countless studies aiming to decipher the connections among the various parts of the human body.

The book contains several tables that again propose the studies of proportion relating to the different parts of the human body.

Intrigued by this macabre side to his master, Leo decides to follow that path.

The culmination of Leonardo's analyses of the relationships between the various parts of the human body is represented by his study of the Vitruvian Man.

A work that is recognised the world over, it is considered by most experts to be the artist's most famous drawing.

The student raises his eyes and encounters the gaze of the Ideal Man in the poster overlooking the bed.

"You knew it!" he says to the perfect man with an irritated tone.

He smiles and continues this train of thought.

The experience da Vinci acquired in all his studies of human proportions is summarized in the creation of the Vitruvian Man, a drawing that has become a universal symbol of perfection.

He puts the book at the foot of the bed, leaving it open at the page showing the famous work.

From the desk drawer he takes out an old case he last used when he was at secondary school.

He picks the book up again and starts to trace lines with a pencil and ruler, directly on the reproduction of the Ideal Man.

This was something that da Vinci was also accustomed to doing.

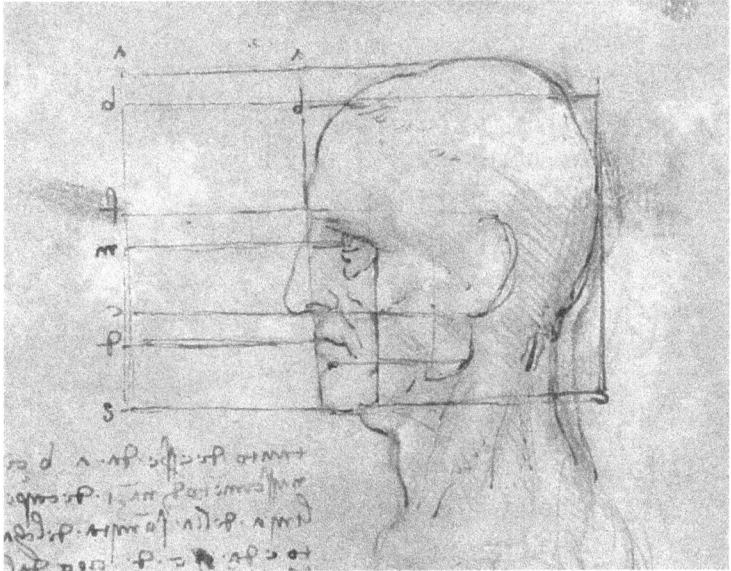

He used this process to illustrate various relationships between the parts.

He observes and measures, traces and cancels, in search of a sign.

The Vitruvian Man is unrecognizable, segmented by the myriad straight lines traced by the student.

The practice is amusing, but it does not lead to any clear and useful result.

Leo stops and once again decides to put in order his thoughts.

"I have to overcome the problem of the perfect length", he declares, repeating the mission of the fourth rebus.

"The universal measurements are observed in the lengths of the figures", he continues recalling the Treatise of the Universal Measurements of Bodies.

"By applying the universal measurements, the master created the perfect Vitruvian Man", he states.

Leo memorizes the three steps and returns to the figure.

Enraptured, he observes its perfect proportions.

At that moment he recalls the definition found on the Internet about the perfect length of a knotted tie.

"The widest part of the tie, which is that immediately before the tip, must lie exactly on the upper edge of the belt."

He returns to the figure and traces a line representing a tie, knotted as defined by the description of the perfect length.

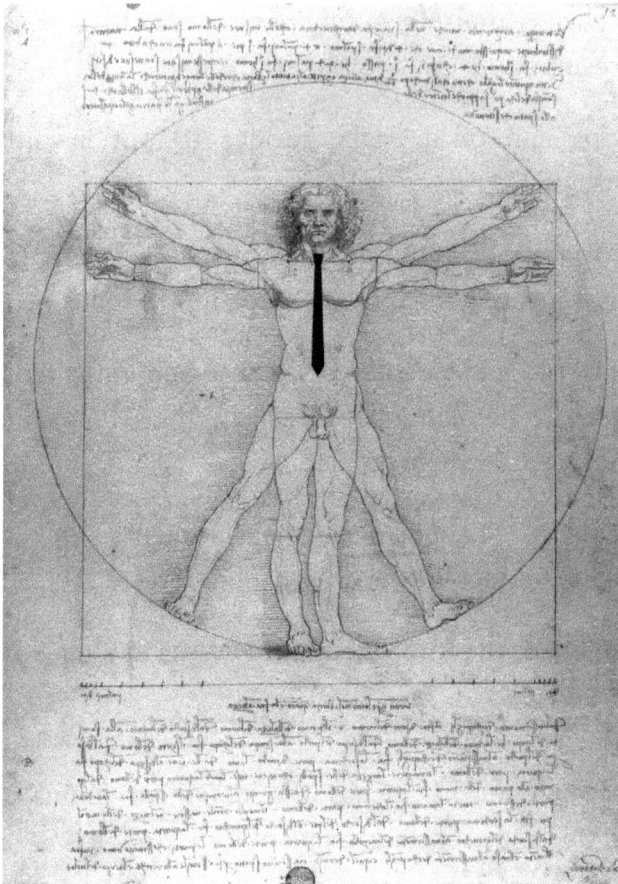

Leonardo observes the man wearing a tie.

A big smile creases his face as he thinks of his master's curses had he seen those changes to his masterpiece.

After five centuries what secret is still concealed behind that perfection?

Which connection is concealed among those proportions?

*** *** ***

"The Da Vinci Code" is Leo's favorite thriller.

A bestseller that has sold over 70 million copies all over the world, largely based on the works of Leonardo da Vinci, could certainly not go unnoticed by an expert of his calibre.

Leo is grateful to the author for having reinforced his master's reputation throughout the world.

A fascinating story surrounded by an aura of Leonardesque mystery that allows the reader to approach Leonardo da Vinci and a number of the issues that he held dear.

One example being the golden number Phi.

After about a hundred pages, Dan Brown introduces this irrational number, mentioning a lesson by Professor Langdon at Harvard University.

Apart from the correlation with the Fibonacci series, the fundamental role of Phi in nature is underlined, a number of examples illustrating where the connection can be found.

Phi has fascinated the human mind over the centuries: characters such as Pythagoras, Kepler and Leonardo da Vinci himself worked on it.

Dan Brown's bestseller testifies to the use of the golden number by the da Vinci in the creation of the Vitruvian Man.

"He was the first to show that the human body literally consists of elements that are linked by a phi relationship" the book reads in the beginning.

"Measure your height and then divide it by the distance from the floor to your navel" is the first example of a Phi relationship.

"Measure the distance from your shoulder to your fingertips and then divide it by the distance from your elbow to your fingertips" the author confirms with another example.

Actually from the numerous anatomical studies found in the manuscripts, numerous drawings were devoted to researching these divine relationships.

The genius's search for perfection is disarming.

Certain studies suggest he was maniacally fascinated by the golden section, quoting incontestable proofs found in a number of his more famous paintings such as the Virgin of the Rocks and the incomparable Mona Lisa.

*** *** ***

Leo's gaze is fixed on his version of his mater's famous male nude wearing a tie.

"1,618033!" he exclaims, recalling the value of the divine proportion.

Who knows whether Phi may help him to solve of the dilemma of perfect length.

However, when you speak about perfection, this golden number always makes an appearance.

"Measure your height and then divide it by the distance from the floor to your navel" he recalls, quoting what Professor Langdon said to his students.

Leo's concentrates on that sentence again, focusing on the presence of the navel, the area where a perfectly knotted tie ends.

He picks up the his ruler and again traces the guideline with his pencil on the reproduction of the master's work in the book.

Carefully he measures the first length.

"118 millimetres" he declares writing the figure down on a corner of the notebook.

He moves the ruler and measures also the second length.

"73 millimetres" he writes down under the first figure.

He reaches out his hand and grabs his mobile phone.

He selects the calculator function and types in the mathematical operation.

"1,617" he reads in surprise.

"Phi!" he declares.

He quickly grabs the bestseller from the second shelf of the bookcase close to the bed.

He leafs through the pages until he finds those dedicated to the golden number.

With his forefinger he follows words.

"Here!" he cries out with a thundering voice, interrupting his reading.

"Measure the distance from your shoulder to your fingertips and then divide it by the distance from your elbow to your fingertips": the second indication dictated by the professor at Harvard University.

With a thoughtful air he dwells on this proposition and casts a glance at the poster.

In his bookcase, mostly devoted to works dealing with Leonardo, there are a number of collections of his anatomical studies, full of drawings and plates facilitating their comprehension.

Among these the student recalls a study by the master that shows precisely the example quoted in The Da Vinci Code.

He puts down the book and goes towards his bookcase.

Quickly he scans the titles of the texts looking for one in particular.

"Et voilà!" he exclaims, grabbing a small volume.

He glances through the pages until he finds the wanted plate he is thinking of.

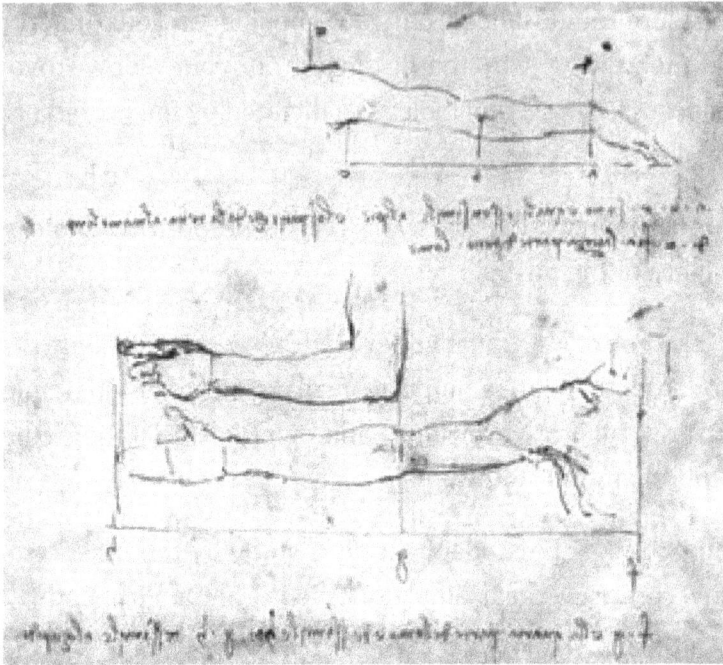

Leo's mind is completely absorbed.

He rubs his eyes.

Again he picks up the ruler and repeats the previous measurements.

He puts the ruler on the figure and notes the first dimension, the distance from the shoulder to the fingertips.

"164 millimetres"

Without moving the ruler, he notes the distance from the elbow to the fingertips.

"101 millimetres"

The calculator leaves no room for doubt.

"1,618!" he confirms the result aloud.

"Phi!" he repeats in astonishment.

The divine proportion represented by Phi unfailingly appears again in this work by da Vinci, thus defining a fundamental element for the perfect execution of his mission.

He takes his old compass out of the case that in the meantime he had carefully replaced.

He goes back to the book and the figure of the man wearing a tie.

With a steady hand he draws a circle with a diameter of the length of the tie.

He stops for a moment to look at the drawing.

"Leonardo da Vinci was left-handed!" the student recalls, observing the open arms of the nude.

Keeping the compass open to the same diameter he then focuses on the left forearm.

"The distance from the elbow to the fingertips", he declares, recalling Dan Brown's example.

Calmly and confidently, he takes the rubber from the case and frees the Ideal Man from his cage of intersecting lines and circles.

He grasps his compass and traces the solution dictated by Phi.

"Voilà!" he exclaims in triumph.

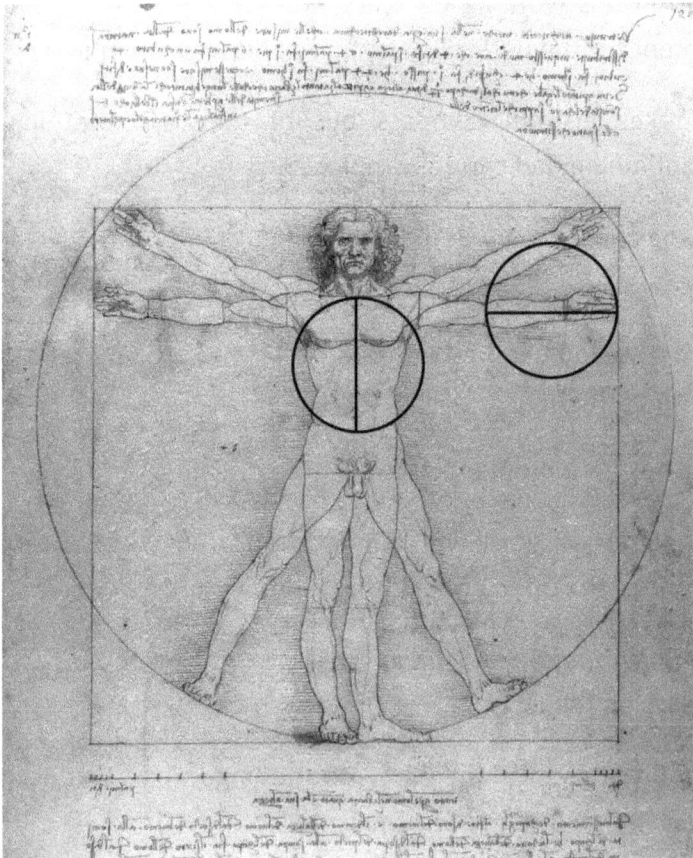

The length of a perfectly knotted tie is the same as the distance between the elbow joint and the fingertips.

"Elementary Watson!" he declares ironically, passing his hand over his tired eyes.

*** *** ***

The notebook is almost full.

Calmly he goes over his notes in search of the keywords that could form the fourth rebus.

He leafs through the pages, and after having drawn the usual four squares he stops to reflect.

The first element is almost obvious.

"The simple knot!"

He recalls the steps that Leonardo recognizes as objective difficulties.

With his ballpoint pen he fill in the first cell:

"Four-in-hand knot".

Proceeding logically, he finds the second element in his scribbles.

"The problem of perfect length."

In the neighbouring cell he writes:

"Perfect length"

Leo continues to apply logic, and recalls Leonardo's studies collected in the known Treatise on the Universal Measurements of Bodies.

A fundamental quotation re-echoes in his mind:

"...In the length of the figures the universal measures are hidden."

His Master's treatise defines a universal theory, which has to be a crucial element.

"Universal measure"

Leonardo completes the third cell.

For the last cell there is no doubt.

The divine number.

Phi.

The golden number suggests to him a correlation between two relationships.

The perfect length of a knotted tie ends at around the navel and reflects the distance between the elbow joint and the fingertips.

Leo carefully completes the list with the final component.

"From the elbow to the fingertips"

four in hand knot

perfect length

universal measure

from the elbow to the fingertips

Leo's search for the solution to the fourth rebus is made easier by the fact that he already knows what he is looking for; that is, the solution to overcoming the problem of knotting a tie to the perfect length.

He observes the four quotations.

The master, after having shown him how to create the perfect knot, wants to specify how to attain the second parameter for a faultless result.

"A kind of universal theory!" the student exclaims.

"A theory that works for everyone!" he states.

Sighing, he pauses silently to think.

*** *** ***

The flowering balconies overlook the square.

The water in the fountain flows clear; spring has arrived bringing with it life and colour.

Smiling children chase after one another, and their mothers sip good coffee while enjoying the warmth of the sun.

The tourists visit the small XIV century church in the Renaissance style, the pride of the small village.

Leo is concentrating on his last rebus; the minutes drag as if they were hours.

The student's mind is feverish; the solution is not far away.

"A universal theory, that works for everybody preparing to knot a tie" he repeats.

After some associations, with a steady and firm voice he exclaims:

"The universal measure for a four-in-hand knot of the perfect length is from the elbow to the fingertips".

He smiles and with an air of triumph he goes out on the balcony to take in the beauty of that spring day.

Last Chapter

Final Rebus

ꙅudɘЯ ⅃ɒniꟻ

"Always remember that truth is more amazing than imagination, you just need to find it."

Charles Fort, 1874-1932, American writer

Leo picks up the sheets of paper scattered over the floor, reassembles the notes and numbers the pages.

There it is, the last page of the precious notebook, most probably its most crucial page.

The sun is shining, it is a lovely day.

With the stack of his precious notes under his arm he goes out to the veranda and sits down on the rocking chair to get a breath of spring air.

The square is full of people, it is the wedding season and the small cathedral lends itself to elegant ceremonies.

People crowd near the main entrance, where the bride and groom are about to cross the fateful threshold.

Leo observes everything from a far, rocking very gently.

An old 1930s Austin Morris, decked out for the wedding, arrives spluttering and, after some minutes dedicated to the taking of photos, it leaves the square with the newly-weds.

The crowd disperses and the old fountain once again dominates the scene.

In front of our student's house, entire families parade, dressed with great elegance for the occasion.

Among them is the numerous Fort family, famous for attending every social event.

Agnese and Luis, the mother and father, of the bride, lead the group.

Behind them come little Martin playing with his sister Jasmine and, a few metres further back, the apprentice Theo joking with his elder brother Alex, a medical student.

Bringing up the rear is Pierino, the grandfather, a popular, jovial figure with a ready smile.

Leo watches as they parade by, and greets them cordially.

As soon as the Fort family disappears around the corner, a comment escapes Leo's lips:

"Everyone is wearing a tie!"

Regardless of age they were all wearing a tie:

An essential ornament to male and even female elegance.

"Everyone is wearing a tie!" he underlines with a satisfied air.

*** *** ***

Leo goes back to studying his notes.

After some minutes spent poring over the stack of sheets, he decides to summarize all the keywords and their solutions on one single sheet.

First Rebus

REBUS - WINDSOR - FASHION - STYLISTS

Solution: Rebus of the necktie knot

Second Rebus

SIMPLE KNOT - POCKET-SIZE - HEXAGON - STEPS

Solution: Steps on a pocketsize hexagon for a simple knot

Third Rebus

BACKWARDS - WITHOUT MIRROR - FOUR - FOR THE DESIGN

Solution: For the design four steps backwards with no mirror

Fourth Rebus

FOUR IN HAND KNOT - PERFECT LENGTH - UNIVERSAL
MEASURE - FROM THE ELBOW TO THE FINGERTIPS

Solution: The universal measure for a four-in-hand knot of
perfect length is from the elbow to the fingertips

Putting down his pen he looks at what he has written.

He smiles, thinking about all the parallels and coincidences that had led him to find and to compose the four rebuses.

"Discovering consists in seeing what everybody has seen and in thinking what nobody has thought" he reaffirms, quoting one of his preferred sayings.

His gaze lingers on that last sheet, in search of the final inspiration.

His eyes open wide, a knowing smile illuminating his face:

"Four, four, four!"

The rocking chair stops.

"Four keywords from four rebuses that lead to four solutions", he confirms observing his notes.

The number four is fundamental to the composition and the decoding of the enigmas.

"The symbol at the base of the hexagon seen in the mirror!" he recalls, speaking out loud.

"The evolution of this symbol through to the number four!" he confirms, referring to the table found on the Internet.

What mystery associated with this number still has to be revealed?

His gaze is fixed on those correlated solutions.

"Four, four, four!" he repeats continuously.

"Four, four, four!"

Motionless with his hands in his hair, he concentrates on his search for intuition.

The rocking chair once again begins to move nervously.

The little birds mark the seconds, equally impatient.

It is midday and the bells of the cathedral echo around the square.

Our student takes no notice.

Silence returns and Leo is still absorbed by his thoughts.

He raises his eyes heavenwards and evidently convinced he exclaims,

"An element is missing!" he returns to his notes and rules aloud:

"A four is missing!" recalling his Master's obsessive search for perfection.

"There are without doubt four elements and not just three."

A shiver runs down his spine.

What can that missing factor be?

Where to find it and what will it be?

Another rebus?

*** *** ***

The pen twirls in his fingers, as if it were incandescent.

He gazes into the distance, in search of the final revelation.

Once again Leo finds himself floundering, lost in the dense jungle of the Leonardesque mind.

"Four words for four rebuses for four solutions!" he repeats, refusing to let it go.

The feeling of something unfinished grips him, a mood he hates.

He takes a calming breath and whispers, "the four keywords provide a solution."

"The four rebuses provide a solution."

He pauses for a moment and then with conviction asks himself:

"Do the four solutions provide a solution?"

Leonardo brightens; enthusiastically he picks up his notes again and rewrites the four solutions in line.

He then examines those solutions and examines them again.

●●●●●●●●●●●●●●●●●●●●●●

Rebus of the tie knot

Steps on a pocket-size hexagon for a simple knot

For the planning four mirror steps
without mirror

The universal measure for a four in hand knot with
the perfect length is from the elbow
to the fingertips

The feeling of being close to the final solution is in the air.

The Renaissance genius has undoubtedly one last stratagem reserved for him.

"Do the four solutions lead to a solution?" he wonders repeatedly.

An obvious connection exists between the four solutions.

The first defines the purpose of the mission, the second precisely indicates the object for the creation of the knot, the third reveals how to make it and the fourth reveals a solution to the problem of perfect length.

Do Leonardo da Vinci's four rebuses lead to a single solution?

Leo is called to a last test.

When you enter da Vinci's world, nothing is left to chance, everything has an explanation.

Leo goes back upstairs to his bedroom and picks up his grandfather's book; perhaps the solution still lies within its pages.

He leafs through it quickly without any clear destination.

Frustrated, he returns to rocking on his chair and starts again from the index.

"Whoa!"

He suddenly stops with the book open at the index and exclaims, "backwards, always backwards!" in reference to Leonardo's mysterious calligraphy.

He returns to the four solutions and quickly rearranges the sentences.

A few moments later with a satisfied air he reads in a steady voice, "the universal measure for the perfect length of a four-in-hand knot is from the elbow to the fingertips. For the design you need four backwards steps with no mirror. Steps on a pocketsize hexagon for a simple knot. The rebus of the tie knot."

The notes fall from his hand, his eyes close and the world around him seems to stop.

"Brilliant!"

Four clues form four rebuses, the four solutions which solve the mystery in a single sentence.

*** *** ***

The flowers on the balconies brighten up the small balconies around the square.

It is the 15th of April 2008 and spring has arrived in all its glory.

Leo has reconstructed and solved the four rebuses that the master had cleverly concealed in his manuscripts.

His grandfather's old book and his sister's gift helped to shed light on the matter, proving to be exceptional guides. His creative mind allowed him to reveal one of the many mysteries that Leonardo da Vinci still hides in his countless pages of notes and works of art.

Leo is sitting on the edge of the old fountain, looking at his reflection in the water.

While he is pleased with having completed the mission entrusted to him, he is not entirely satisfied.

A fundamental detail leaves him proud but feeling incomplete, he anticipated the date of consignment that was supposed to coincide with his birthday on the 8th of December 2008.

He raises his eyes and while observing the horizon, his face breaks into a smile.

"The 15th of April", he exclaims with pleasure.

"Happy birthday master!"

Afterword

$$\frac{4node}{\partial bon4}$$

"A well-tied tie is the first serious step in life."

Oscar Wilde, 1854-1900, Irish writer and poet

'

The necktie is a clothing accessory symbolizing male elegance.

The six hundred million men who habitually knot a tie around their necks are rarely aware of the symbolic, magical and mythological background to this seemingly insignificant act.

The tie was born as a simple piece of cloth that the Roman legionaries wore around their necks for hygienic or climatic reasons.

Several centuries later, the Croatian knights recruited by Louis XIV, wore it as a kind of scarf during the Thirty Years' War.

A few decades later, the French appropriated the idea; hence the origin of the French term cravat, derived from the Croatian "hrvat."

In 1661, Louis XIV established the post of the King's "tie maker": a gentleman entrusted with the task of helping the sovereign to embellish and knot his tie.

In 1925, the American Jesse Langsdorf patented the modern-day tie, made with three pieces of cut on the bias fabric.

Over the course of centuries the tie has assumed ever-greater importance, becoming a true mark of elegance and refinement and establishing a unique role.

It expresses the wearer's personality and becomes an instrument of great importance in social relationships.

Despite the necktie's ubiquity, it is still surrounded by an aura of mystery; there are many men who cannot tie a decent tie, even with the simplest knot, the four-in-hand.

In the late 1990s, two Cambridge University researchers, Thomas Fink and Yong Mao, used mathematical models to show that a conventional tie can be knotted in 85 different ways.

Every knot has its own distinctive characteristic, but all share the common denominator of simple elegance.

The art of tying a tie is expressed in most cases through the following types of knots:

Four-in-Hand Knot (simple knot)

Tied in four steps, the name derives from the 19th century London gentlemen's Four-in-Hand Club.

Half-Windsor Knot

Tied in six steps, it takes its name from its older "cousin", the Windsor knot.

St. Andrew Knot

Tied in seven steps, this unusual knot makes the tie protrude slightly from the neck before hanging on the chest.

Windsor Knot

Tied in eight steps, this knot became popular in the 1930s when the Duke of Windsor began to prefer larger knots.

Balthus Knot

Tied in nine steps, this very large knot was devised by the 20th century Surrealist painter of the same name.

It is now essential to be familiar with at least the most well-known knot.

Most commonly known as simple knot and tied in four basic steps.

Ideal for the majority of ties and for almost all shirt collars, it is slim and tapered and should not be too triangular.

After having invented, drawn, created and prophesied manifold devices, do you really think that Leonardo da Vinci would not have considered this curious and mysterious aspect of a man's life?

Faithfully respecting certain elements and parallels concealed in his manuscripts, by combining the four solutions to the rebuses, Leo created the object that solves the mystery, providing a key to mastering the dilemma: a pocket-size support of hexagonal shape on which to execute four simple steps.

Leonardo da Vinci defines a universal point of departure for the execution of the four steps in the knotting of a tie of the perfect length for everyone. Moreover, by taking his cue from his enigmatic handwriting, he simplifies the operation to the extent that a mirror is no longer necessary.

To discover and to order this Da Vinci's intuition please connect to:

https://4node.ecwid.com/

INDEX

BIBLIOGRAPHY

85 modi di annodare la cravatta

Science and aesthetics of the Knot - Thomas Fink and Yong Mao - Publishing House Bompiani Etas Fabbri Sonzogno

Il Codice Da Vinci

Omnibus Series - Dan Brown - Translated by Riccardo Valla - Mondadori 2004

"Discovering consists in seeing what everybody has seen and in thinking what nobody has thought. "

Albert Szent-Györgyi, 1893-1986, Hungarian scientist